ALSO BY DR. PHIL McGRAW

Life Strategies

Life Strategies Workbook

Relationship Rescue

Relationship Rescue Workbook

Self Matters

The Self Matters Companion

The Ultimate Weight Solution

The Ultimate Weight Solution Cookbook

The Ultimate Weight Solution Food Guide

Family First: Your Step-by-Step Plan for Creating a Phenomenal Family

The Family First Workbook: Specific Tools, Strategies and Skills for Creating a Phenomenal Family

Love Smart

Find the One You Want—Fix the One You Got

Dr. Phil McGraw

DOUBLEDAY LARGE PRINT HOME LIBRARY EDITION

Free Press

New York London Toronto Sydney

This Large Print Edition, prepared especially for Doubleday Large Print Home Library, contains the complete, unabridged text of the original Publisher's Edition.

FREE PRESS
A Division of Simon & Schuster, Inc.
1230 Avenue of the Americas
New York, NY 10020

Manufactured in the United States of America

Library of Congress Cataloging-in-Publication Data is available

ISBN: 0-7394-6286-5
ISBN: tk

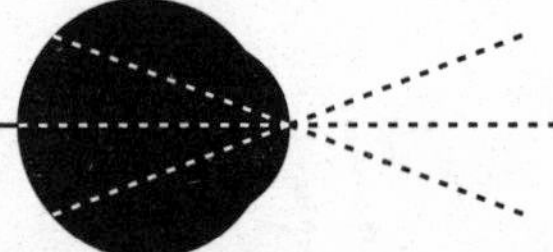

This Large Print Book carries the Seal of Approval of N.A.V.H.

To Robin, my loving wife of twenty-nine years, who knows me from the inside out and loves me anyway!

Every day I wake up by your side is a day worth living.

You are the relationship model.

Acknowledgments

Robin, you are the culmination of what anyone reading this book would pray for. Our relationship has been the crowning achievement in my life and continues to be to this very day. You have loved me when I have been hard to love, celebrated our love each and every day and mothered our wonderful children. You never, ever stopped being the girl I married even though you have become the woman to whom I am married. In our relationship we have embraced every adventure and have been advocates in each other's balcony of life from day one. You taught me about what makes relationships work, and without you I would not be the good parts of the person I am today. Thanks for never complaining about the long hours, solitary book writing and endless challenges. We are just getting started!

Jay and Jordan, thanks for always believing in your dad and being proud of what I do and how I do it. You boys and your mom keep me focused, laughing and feeling good about getting up every day.

And to my mother and father, who unfailingly modeled honoring commitments with fifty-plus years of marriage, I thank you for keeping it together for yourselves as well as for all of us. And especially to my mother for being such a great supporter of me as a husband and father since my father's death, and such a loving grandmother to our boys. That family relationship bond has had lasting strength as Deana, Donna, Brenda and I have stayed close in our own relationship. And to the three sisters, thanks for spoiling me early and giving me the scoop on girls when I had absolutely no clue. If a man's worth is measured by the love in his family, I am the richest man in the world.

Oprah, thank you for your friendship and for your endless belief and support of my work. You make this world a better place. Your vision for my platform on television and in print has challenged me every day since it began, and I thank you for that. You have made a difference not only in this country, but also in the cradle of humanity by leading by example and living with completeness and honesty.

Thank you to G. Frank Lawlis, Ph.D., who has been my mentor, colleague and friend for thirty years. You have always been there when I needed you and are always willing to help, especially with the most complex, pivotal challenges. Your insight and enthusiasm are absolutely invaluable, and I am grateful for both. Your encyclopedic knowledge of human functioning is also immeasurable.

And to Scott Madsen, who always merits mention: As usual, you have dedicated your days, nights and weekends when you had plenty of other places to be. You have never uttered the word "no" and for that I give you my deepest appreciation. Thanks for always being there for me and mine over the last thirty-five years. When I go head down and tail up on projects such as this one, you always keep all the fires burning.

Thank you also to Bill Dawson. You are a mind among minds and a trusted and valued friend. Your support on the business and personal front for the last fifteen-plus years has meant and does mean more than you can imagine. Our conversations across the endless hours on everything from religion to Emma the pup are a great refuge. Thanks for always having my back on every front.

If ever there was a crew to have by your side it is the one with me day in and day out. Terri Wood, Carla Pennington, Kandi Amelon and Angie Kraus, you have all been relentlessly committed to making *Dr. Phil* the TV show live up to our internal challenge of creating the best hour on television and the highest and best use of the medium. There isn't anything that can't be accomplished with the "Four Tops" in your corner! Then there is the world's premier publicist and bad boy himself, Chandler Hayes. You are my eyes and ears, and I couldn't walk the walk without you. Thanks for believing so deeply in what we do.

A huge thank you also to Carolyn Reidy, Dominick Anfuso and the Simon & Schuster/Free Press group for always believing in the importance of my message. Your passion in making sure that the words contained herein make it into every pair of hands in America is deeply appreciated.

To Jan Miller and Shannon Miser-Marven, my agents at Dupree/Miller, your passion for my message over the years has been continually uplifting. You two are my literary "feminine side," and you make my books so much better because of your hard and tireless work, not to mention making them be on time! Your entire team, including Alia Brinkman, Jennifer Holder, Annabelle Baxter and Nena Madonia with their all important research and organization made this book possible, made it fun and ensured its relevance.

Thank you to Leah Furman, Michele Bender and Bill Kelley, who brought their unique talents to this project. Your involvement was essential, and because of your dedication and work, this book is improved. You were true professionals in every sense of the word, and for that I am grateful.

Contents

Love Smart

Find the One You Want—
Fix the One You Got

1

Your GPS: Great Partner Search

True Love is the only heart disease that is best left to "run on"—the only affection of the heart for which there is no help, and none desired.

MARK TWAIN, *NOTEBOOK*

People—you, me, all of us—are pretty much social animals. Left to our own devices, we tend to seek one another's company—mentally, physically, spiritually. You can put a small number of people in a large space, and in a short time they will cluster, seeking to see, hear and touch one another.

Just being around other people doesn't seem to be enough. On the day-to-day level, we, as human beings, tend to pair off seeking more than to just "hang out" with random bipeds. We seem to need to fall in love, be in love and share love. Since we all seem to kind of want the same things, you would think it would be relatively easy to pair up and meet each other's mutual needs. But have you ever noticed that the smarter and more sophisticated we become, the harder we seem to make those parts of our life that should be the easiest? I have people tell me all the time that for some reason, they just can't seem to find another human being who is willing to share the two little words "we" and "us," let alone put their boots under their bed and start filing joint tax returns. They tell me that they just can't get a date and if they do, it's either with some mouth-breather they hope they never see again or a decent guy who won't call back, either because he doesn't want to or is afraid his wife might find out. As a result, they just sit around watching the drapes fade.

As a few excerpts from your e-mails and letters show, at least most of you are keeping a sense of humor:

In all honesty, at this point in my life, being desperate seems like the good old days. I was on a blind date two weekends ago, and we couldn't meet at a club because being in a place that served liquor would violate his parole. I don't need someone to throw me a life preserver. I need someone to pull me out of the "lonely waters" and perform CPR.

My last blind date picked me up at my high-rise. We walked out to where a number of cars were parked at the curb. He opened the car door, put me in and walked around the back of the car, got into his car and left! I was sitting in some stranger's car! I will hunt him down if it takes the rest of my life!

The last date I had was with a computer guy who spent hours telling me why "Windows ruled!" By the time he was done, I was just looking for one to jump out of.

The last time I had a second date, I think that he actually called me by mistake and was too embarrassed to admit it! He ate dinner like he was in an eating contest, rushed out like he was double-parked and I was back home before my dog even knew I was gone. Help!

I'm embarrassed to say it, but the other day, a guy leaned out of his car and yelled, "Nice legs!" and I almost said, "Thanks for noticing" and asked him for his number. I've got a job, better than average body and face and I dress nicely. What am I doing wrong?

I need to find someone fast before I become one of those women who dresses up her pets and calls them her "children." I am too young to be the "Crazy cat woman" that scares the neighborhood kids. Please help before it is too late for me and my cats!

I quit! This one accountant at work is built like a footstool and smells like peanut butter, but she came in Monday with an engagement ring the size of a grape! I, on the other hand, sorted coupons all weekend! She's calling friends telling them she's planning a wedding; I'm calling mine and telling them that Tuesday I'm planning on getting forty cents off a can of Pledge!

Your personal situation may be better or worse than some of those ladies' but either way, it's time to shake it up and get what you truly want. To do that you're going to have to learn to Love Smart.

If you can't find the guy you want or don't know how to fix the guy you got, you and I are about to change that in a major way. If you're up at night wondering why everybody around you, *except you,* is in great relationships, getting engaged, getting married, having kids and zooming right along in life, then you and I are about to change *that* in a major way. If you're not finding that special someone who can light you up from the inside out, you are getting shortchanged, and we're definitely going to fix that. Something isn't right. Something is out of whack. What makes it even worse is that I believe with great certainty that this special someone *does* exist. He is out there. You may have already met him. You may even have a relationship with him but just can't move it to the next level, or maybe you're married to him but the sizzle has started to fizzle.

To get the relationship you want, you have to be willing to take an honest, even brutal, look at what's going on and what's going wrong. You have to be willing to change what you are doing.

Just a note to be sure that I'm very clear on one thing: I am about to let you in on some secrets and strategies, assuming that you have decided that you want to find the right man for you. I do not now believe, nor have I ever believed, that any woman has to be married or have a man in her life in order to be whole, complete or vitally alive. Having a man in your life is something that can be good, if you find the right one. It's healthy to want and have a boyfriend or husband (not at the same time, of course). But this is *not* something that you *need* or *must have*. Getting married is *not* something you *must* do.

Assuming that finding the right man is what you want, the task of creating a strong and rewarding relationship in this fast-paced day and time in our highly transient society—with its high divorce rate—may sound intimidating or even overwhelming. Let me assure you, it doesn't have to be. In fact, what we're about to do is going to be more fun than the law should allow. How exciting, how much fun is it to know that each and every day could be the day when you meet the person of your dreams, the person with whom you will spend the rest of your life? You never know if the next business meeting you have, the next customer you serve or the next corner you turn will put you in front of that very person! This makes life exhilarating; I don't care who you are! Especially if all of a sudden you are no longer stumbling along aimlessly, but instead have the skills, abilities, plans and strategies to make it happen! You are about to master the art of relating. You are about to get your relationship "black belt." Then you are going to look back at what you used to do and just shake your head.

I want you to CLAIM what you want, and it is pretty simple to envision:

CREATE a clear vision of what you want
LOCATE the person you want to do it with
ATTRACT him like a magnet
INSPIRE him to want what you want long term
MARRY him and get busy being happy!

Let me start us off by telling you two things that I know for absolute, drop-dead certain. First: if you do not have what you truly want in a relationship, then you are right, something is seriously wrong. But here's the important part: What is wrong is not you. I repeat, the problem is *not* you. You are not a bad person. You are not failing to get a wonderfully rewarding relationship because you are not worthy of it. In fact, I believe, to the absolute core of my soul, that you are about to discover a huge secret, in fact, I believe it is the best-kept secret in your life: YOU. This secret is not only being hidden from the people you see every day, bond with or dream of marrying, it is being kept from you.

The second thing I know for absolute, drop-dead certain is that you are not thinking right or playing the game well; otherwise you would have what you want. We'll deal with that in Chapter 4, "Single—There Are No Accidents," because you are a deserving and quality potential relationship partner, but you apparently don't know how to get in the game or play the game once you do.

And yes, it is a game. Somehow or another, people have decided that looking for love is some hugely serious process that must be approached with reverence and decorum. I guess I shouldn't be so surprised since seriousness is usually associated with desperate situations and "desperation" is a word I often hear from both men and women regarding their love lives. I agree that selecting a life partner and making the decision to walk the aisle is a decision of gravity and deserves the utmost in contemplation, prayer and consideration. But, the process that gets you there *is* a game and a game that has to be played loose and fun if you want to win. You've got to play the game without sweaty palms or you will never get what you are looking for.

Saying that dating and relating is, at least in the beginning, a game does not mean that it is trivial or frivolous. Make no mistake; I'm talking about making a major change in your life, specifically your love life. It's time to be a winner. It's time to start being a bride instead of a bridesmaid.

Think about it, the problem has to be something besides you. Don't you know women who are, in your humble opinion, not as interesting as you, not as smart as you, not as loving and caring and giving as you, not as cute or attractive as you, but yet they have a great relationship partner while you sit at home talking to your houseplants? Why? Maybe they just got blind lucky, but I'm betting they have what they want and what you wish you had because they know how to play the game better than you do.

I know that there are also women out there that you just love to hate, because they seem to have it all going on. They're young, fit, stick-thin, energetic and cute. You're thinking, "How do I compete with *that*?" You stand in your bathroom looking in the mirror and saying, "Look at my hair! Look at my hips! I've got legs like stumps! My eyes are too far apart! This is the genetic betrayal that is my legacy! I am destined to die alone!" Well, snap out of it! I can promise you that you don't want or need to be some beauty-queen model that spends her days on the runway. She may very well be home starving, or puking up the dinner she just pigged out on, looking in the mirror and saying the very same things you say or worse. Besides, I can't tell you how many men I've heard look at those women and say "Good grief! I've seen more meat on antlers! She needs to spend a little more time at the buffet."

If you're sitting at home dogging on yourself with an endless list of self-critical put-downs, then I guarantee that other people, including men, are going to find it very difficult to see value in you because you are hiding it so well. You're going to have to understand yourself and know yourself—and, as strange as it sounds, before he ever falls in love with you, *you* are going to have to fall in love with *you*.

Here's how this is all going to start. To get you where you want to go, we're going to absolutely rewrite the script of your life, and you're going to be the star. We are going to identify, describe and embrace the "Character of You" in Chapter 3—and that character is going to be the star in your life. And it's no longer a one-woman show. We are going to identify your leading man in Chapter 2, "The Character of Him." We are going to define both characters in terms of personality, physical traits, values, beliefs and every other important characteristic so you know exactly who you are and what you're looking for. You have to know you from the inside out, you have to recognize who you are and you have to commit to a "defined product" of how you will present yourself in the social arena. The "defined product" is the best possible you that is available within the range of who you are, and that's the horse you're going to ride all the way home—all the way down the aisle. No more trying to be all things to all people. No more trying to guess what some man wants and struggling to morph yourself into it. You are going to be the best you can be, rather than somebody you are not, and I promise you that will be more than enough to create the love you want.

You are going to have to discover those parts of yourself that any man would want. Parts that you don't recognize now, and embrace them. It should be obvious if you are sabotaging yourself. I live in Hollywood now, and every other person I meet is an agent. They're all out there trying to promote their undiscovered "star." Can you imagine if they tried to do that by repeating the kind of things about their future star that you repeat to yourself about your self? Imagine if they stepped up and said, "Hey, I got this old hide of a woman client that I want you to meet. She's sort of drab and boring, doesn't get out much and isn't very interesting, but, I don't know, maybe you'll like her. She's certainly available. It's been so long since she had a date that her clothes have gone out of style." I'm sure that sounds pretty ridiculous when you think about somebody describing another person that way. If so, why doesn't it sound ridiculous to you when you describe yourself that way?

You will not succeed in the highly competitive dating game unless you are *convinced* that you are absolutely fabulous. REMEMBER: You cannot fake fabulous. You have to *be* fabulous and know that you *are* fabulous! I'm going to show you how to discover the fabulous parts of you in Chapter 5, "Your Inner Bride," and I don't mean just pumping you full of sunshine with a bunch of rah, rah, power-of-positive-thinking. I mean getting you to have a full appreciation of the unique individual that you are.

There are 100 million single people in America, representing 44 percent of the population. Half of them are men. People get happily married every day. If marriage is what you want, you can, with hard work and candor, create some exciting options.

Once you acquire the skills and abilities necessary to play the dating game and play it powerfully, results are going to come.

So I'm telling you that your problem finding the right guy has nothing to do with your personal worth or value. It is not even a problem of superficial things like your attractiveness. It *is,* however, a problem, rooted in what you are doing and not doing. That probably sounds like the bad news. But I think it is just more good news, because you can change your behavior. We are about to help you do that. We're about to solve your problem, and it isn't going to involve a season pass to the plastic surgeon or the shrink. You can find that special someone who you know is right for you. You can create a relationship that will scratch every itch you have and fulfill the dreams you had since you were a little girl. I am totally serious. If you will embrace the concepts that I'm about to lay out, adopt the behaviors that I'm going to prescribe and employ the strategies that we're going to create together: problem solved! It doesn't matter if you're in a situation where you can't get a date, can't get the right date, can't get the man in your life to pop the question or can't get the man you married to pull his head out and honor and cherish you. You and I are going to change all that—and what's more, we are going to have an absolute ball doing it. It's time to get what you want!

I don't want you to panic, and I certainly don't want you to feel like you've already missed the bus, but it *is* time to stop burning daylight and to recognize that this is no dress rehearsal. This is Show Time. Think about it: You're only going to live a total of about 25,000 days at the most. That's just 3,900 weeks! If you're in your thirties, you've only got about 12,000 days—1,800 weeks—left, or 1,800 weekends to turn to your cat and say, "Let's check out what's on Animal Planet." Did you get that? You can measure what's left of your life in weeks! Weeks! The truth is, life can and will come and go in a hurry. It's time to start playing the game to win, and that means that you have to prepare. I have often said the difference between winners and losers is winners do things losers don't want to do. It's time to act like a winner.

Here's a bottom-line truth: Dating as you know it is simply one of the most inefficient, nonproductive, haphazard and hit-or-miss ways to try and achieve one of the most important objectives of your entire life. I mean, give me a break, how lame is typical date rhetoric: "So what's your sign? Can you believe all this rain? Did you see *People* magazine this week?" Jeez Louise! I would be looking for a rope to hang myself with before the appetizers arrived. It's a wonder we haven't disappeared as a species, owing to a shutdown of procreation. If you go into the dating arena, like most people, with no training, no insight, no plan and no strategy, you're like a missile without a guidance system. You're like a car without a steering wheel. You're just out there hoping that Mr. Right jumps up on the hood and knocks on your windshield screaming, "Hey, stop! It's me, it's me, you found me!" I suspect that by the way you've probably been playing the game so far, you would just hit the washers and wipers and scrape him off like a bug. You may have already run over him twice! (If that's the case, let's hope he's not a lawyer!)

I want us to be proactive like the vulture sitting up on a telephone line who looks at the other vulture and says, "Forget this waiting. I'm going to go kill something." I want you to be that way. I want you out there making things happen. In order to do that, you need to have a clear strategy and you need to have the skills to execute that strategy. From getting noticed all the way to closing the deal. Chapter 9, "Infrared Dating," will show you how to cut to the chase with potential partners so you're not sitting there sorting Jell-O boxes for eight months in a relationship that never had a future, never had a chance to breathe on its own beyond a few random good times. I am going to talk to you about where to go to expose yourself to potential partners (whether it's at a nightclub, gym, church or online dating, which we'll cover in Chapter 8, "Fishing with a Net"), know who is for real and who is a waste of time and how to conduct yourself when you get there in Chapter 7, "Your Man Plan."

The truth is that effective dating is tough. I wonder how men and women ever get together to begin with, let alone stay together. There couldn't be two more different "species" on the face of the planet. I can remember that when I was young, I thought all cats were girls and all dogs were boys, and that's why they didn't get along. I had that straightened out for me after a time, but I have to say that after all these years have passed I've decided that I might have been a lot closer to the truth when I was five!

My dad, a career psychologist, used to say that men didn't have a clue about women. The day I married Robin, he laughed and said there were two times in any man's life that he will be confused by women: before he gets married and after he gets married. I got the feeling that he had learned this from painful life experiences, not out of a book!

Men and women may not understand each other as much as we would like, but as a man I do understand how men think. I intend to be like your "friend at the factory." In Chapter 6, "Your Guy-Q," we figure out how to get men to do what you want them to do and not do what you don't want them to do. My knowledge is experiential in that I am a man and it's observational in that I have spent a lot a time around a lot of guys, some of them hound dogs, some of them not. But you are going to have to understand what makes a man tick, why he's afraid of commitment if he is, what it is he wants and what it's going to take for him to recognize the value in you. You're going to have to understand men, if you expect to take on a new last name or hyphenate that one you got.

I'm going to focus not on esoteric differences, but on the things that really matter to you in your quest to find a man to share your life with, such as how to get men to make marriage a priority, how to overcome their apparent fear of commitment and how to best ensure that they value you as a woman and treat you with dignity and respect.

This will be no easy deal, because there is a huge difference between men and women—specifically regarding the priority to create a committed relationship and a marriage. Think about it. Little girls grow up playing dress-up and having fantasy weddings. They grow up acting a wedding out, planning the details, putting towels on their heads as pretend veils. Do you think men do that? We've all heard about the little girls who march their Barbies down "the aisle" so they can marry their brothers' G.I. Joes. But have you ever heard of a little boy who stole his sister's Barbie so she could marry his poor, lonely G.I. Joe? Have you ever seen a little boy tear up tissue paper and put it on a doll's head, pretending that it is a veil?

So what do you do when there is such a difference of priorities? The answer is that you have to create motivation in your man; you have to create a sense of desire and urgency. As with a lot of other things, doing that is easy when you know how and it's like trying to get water to run uphill when you don't. A lot of men have told me over the years that when it comes to dating or being in a relationship, they feel they are being hunted, tracked and targeted to become husbands. This is a little disconcerting. You know how women always say that men are interested in only one thing. Well, let me assure you, men have their version of that story—men believe that you too are interested in only one thing. The goal is to create a sense of urgency without the perception of pressure. I guess there is certain symmetry there because both men and women believe there is a definite cause-and-effect relationship involved in what each is perceived to want! And while marriage may in fact be your primary objective, you just really aren't that much of a threat to a man who thinks he values his "freedom"—because, frankly, I think most women just simply aren't very good at closing the deal. Let's face it: If you have no technique, it's time that we fix that. I'm going to show you how in Chapter 10, "Bag 'em, Tag 'em, Take 'em Home." If you're going to make a real connection with a man, not just trap him, but capture his heart, mind and soul AND make him like it—you're going to need some serious know-how. Urgency without pressure is the goal. Specifically you need to know how to find the right man, attract him, motivate him and marry him. That's blunt, but if that's what you want to know that's what we are going to do and have a good time while we're doing it.

If you're already married to a man, and you just want to relight those fires and keep them burning, you too are going to need the serious know-how from Chapter 11, "The State of Your Union."

This book is not about finding Mr. Right Now; it is about finding Mr. Right. I say that because there is a huge difference between being able to get a man to say "I do" at a given moment in time and being able to get him (or you) to say, *"I am* happily married for the long term." If your goal is to get to "I do," then you have a different set of standards from what you have if your goal is "I am." To get to "I do" you just tell a man whatever he wants to hear just to get him to say those words and walk down the aisle. You can then focus on the important issues of arguing with your mom about caterers and photographers. But you are not going to be happily married. Yes, you'll get your dream day, but you will fall short of a dream life. If you're looking for more than a year of wedding planning, a fancy dress and a big party; if what you want is a solid relationship based on a foundation of love and caring; if what you want is more than just an "I *do*" but a sincere and emphatic "I *am* happily married," then closing the deal is not about finding any man but about creating a relationship with the right man that is good for the both of you. Now let's get started.

2

The Character of Him

On the one hand we'll never experience childbirth, on the other hand we can open our own jars.

BRUCE WILLIS

The writing is on the wall: Your biological clock is ticking so loudly that your neighbors can hear it; your stomach probably turns at the thought of going to another loud, smoke-filled bar just so that a bunch of guys can ogle you like a twenty-ounce porter-house (with a baked potato on the side); and you're thinking, "If I have to go on so much as one more date with another hair-gelled, sunglasses-at-night-wearing pretty boy who spends more on clothes than I do, I'm going to throw up in my mouth." If that's you and you want off the dating circuit, it is time for you to stop acting like a rank amateur, just looking and waiting for some random guy to choose you. **If you're going to love smart, then you're going to have to date smart.** You've been there, done that—it's time for the next phase of your life to begin.

On the other hand, you may be the type who never goes on dates or to clubs. You're an outsider who can't even figure out how to get into the game long enough to be sick of it, much less how you'll ever find the guy you want. You've watched *Sex and the City* and thought it's a fairy tale—"No way are there women out there who are dating as much as these four," not when your last date was when the macarena topped the charts! I'm with you there. Like so much of what you see on television or on the big screen, that show and others like it don't reflect any world I've ever heard of. That is probably why so many people watch them, wishing life really could be that way. Maybe you're like that. Maybe you've lived vicariously through every movie star and feel-good movie you can think of and you've had it up to your bloodshot eyeballs with watching the world go by.

Whether you're a "been there done that" woman or an "I don't even know how to get there" woman doesn't really matter much. Both kinds of women are in the same boat. Whichever you are, you haven't been able to get a foothold on a quality relationship with a quality guy. And that is not because you're a loser, but because you haven't really gone at this like a winner—with the plan and skill set necessary to maximize your chances.

Men should be like Kleenex—soft, strong and disposable.

CHER

So here we go. Let's get down to what this chapter is all about—writing a character profile of "him." Who exactly, precisely, specifically do you consider to be a quality guy? Figuring this out now doesn't mean that you shouldn't be fluid and open to change, but it helps to at least start with some objective in mind. I'm not going to try to turn you into some high-maintenance, hyperpicky naysayer. I just want to help you stop kissing frogs and start finding your man. Here is where we set some standards and start learning to reject those guys who fall so far below the bar that they make inmates look good. This is all about beginning with the end in mind (as Dr. Stephen Covey would say) and not bothering with a hound dog when what you really want is someone with a pedigree—or at the very least, someone who's housebroken and won't gnaw on the furniture!

And, boy, are there a lot of hound dogs out there. A woman was telling me recently about this guy who was coming on superstrong and trying to sweep her off her feet at a resort in Aspen, Colorado. To hear her tell his story, James Bond was modest in comparison. She said if he'd been any more full of himself, she would have had to get a table for three instead of two just so his ego wouldn't have to stand.

He was apparently regaling her with tales of all the status symbols he so fondly called his own: his Porsche parked out front; his new Range Rover, which was being hand-waxed back at his garage; his gold Rolex, which he kept flashing ad nauseam just in case she might miss it. He discussed his

Prada shoes and his art collection. No shame—his high-rise condo, his sailboat in the marina, he left nothing out. The guy had *no* shame—like a waiter proud of himself for having perfectly recited the specials he wrapped it up with a smug look that seemed to say, "So what do you think?" She looked him dead in the eye and said, "Want to know what I think? I think you've got a lot of bills, Slick. You either have more money than brains or you are in hock up to your eyeballs." Totally unimpressed, she had been sitting there the whole time wondering, "What's the deal with boys and their toys! In a million years I wouldn't spend money on that junk! Jeez, what about a college fund for my children, a retirement account, savings and a husband who spends more on his family than his golf clubs? That's what I want!"

Look, I understand the appeal of the hound dog. I've heard that ol' boys' song and dance many times before. You have to understand: The qualities that initially attract you to a man are not necessarily the ones that will make him a good long-term partner. If you are genuinely looking to settle down and you still don't understand that the guy chasing you may not be the person you want raising your children or being there for you through thick and thin, then it's time we get you a plan, an emotional compass, and start changing your selection criteria immediately.

Does that mean there's anything wrong with somebody who's fun on a date, a good dancer, handsome and supercool? Absolutely not. In fact, you may consider those conditions to be necessary and they may be, but that certainly does not mean those traits are sufficient to sustain what you're looking for.

I don't mean to make this sound like a job with no fun, spontaneity or intrigue—because, as I said in Chapter 1, this should be an exciting process. But we might as well make sure you are enjoying yourself with the right kind of guys, that is, those who have at least some chance of being "the one." That means you need to stop spending time around people who you absolutely, positively, drop-dead know for sure are not going to lead you anywhere. Don't go barhopping just because you are scared to be alone.

♥♡

If what you are looking for is a meaningful, committed partner, then you are going to have to stay on the relationship highway and quit going down the doesn't-call-you-back dirt roads, the better-than-nothing dead-end streets, and the he-ain't-much-but-he's-mine detours.

If you want what you want when you want it and what you want is a real, no-kidding, quality partner and when you want it is now (or yesterday before noon) instead of five years from now or never, then you don't want to confuse aimless social activity with social productivity.

Here's an attitude adjustment for you: Decide right now that you would rather be happy alone than miserable with somebody else. Decide that you will not choose some guy out of fear that you may not get a better choice later. For example, if you know a guy who drinks too much, has a difficult personality and hates kids, he's no good to you unless you're writing a country song. He may be fun for the night, but there's no chance for a future because he has deal-breaking characteristics or values. And you need to be paying attention to those and hitting the door even if it means going home alone.

Debbie is a thirty-four-year-old woman I know who was dating a guy she was ridiculously attracted to. We're talking catnip. I mean, she could and did easily spend hours just staring at his picture and daydreaming about how sexy he was. But despite all that mooning, she held a part of herself back and never let herself get too attached. She kept her balance by seeing other people because she had been burned by charming "pretty boys" before and knew that once the sexual attraction settled down, she would be stuck with a handsome and charming guy who was also extremely immature, controlling, noncommittal and irresponsible.

Wasted time! He was nothing but a distraction, stealing valuable time that could have been productively spent with real possibilities. She left him far behind.

If you haven't stopped to give your needs and wants some serious thought, you probably wouldn't know Mr. Right if he walked up to you wearing a name tag. You don't fit with everybody, and not everybody fits with you. There are people out there who will drive you crazy and vice versa. I want to make sure that you have a clear vision of what you want and what you don't want—what you absolutely cannot live with versus "Yes, this is the foundation on which I can build a future."

Here's a hint: What you want is not necessarily Brad Pitt, George Clooney, Gandhi and Bill Gates all rolled into one. After all, as he gets older, he's likely to have Bill Gates's looks and Gandhi's money. You're not going for some dream guy here, because going for a dream guy is a good way to excuse yourself from the game—just set the bar so high that nobody measures up, then shrug your shoulders and say, "That's why I'm alone." No, we are going to get in there and be realistic and find somebody who has a chance of being the right kind of guy. Then we'll create the right kind of experience.

Deal Breakers 101

When describing the Character of Him, identifying what you don't want is as important as identifying what you do want. So, first let's make a quick list of what you don't want and absolutely will not tolerate. These are what I call deal breakers. They are the traits, qualities and characteristics that go against your core values: that set of ideals and beliefs—such as honesty, justice and courage—which you use to judge character and moral fiber and which serve to maintain your integrity. If someone has characteristics that clearly run counter to this core value system, it doesn't much matter how cute you think he is or how nice a car he drives. If there is something about him that you know will drive you out of your ever-loving mind in no time at all, then you need to address that issue right here and now.

Trust me, if you're dealing with a guy who is broken in some major way, tell him to get help, give him the name of a good counselor but don't take that on when you still have an option to choose wisely. That may sound harsh, but you are looking for a healthy, functional partner who is uniquely compatible with you. You are not a halfway house, you aren't Ms. Fix-It and, anyway, he already has a mother! If you are married or deeply in love or both and your partner has developed serious flaws and problems, that's another thing. You are at a different stage. You've made a commitment to be there for him, to support and guide him, to patiently help him heal what ails him, though not to the point of being self-destructive.

Taking on big problems, however, is just not smart. Don't think you are going to succeed by being a rescuer and earning your place. It is tough enough to merge two lives without those kinds of problems. You are worthy of a fully functioning, healthy, quality mate. You are going to have to start making different choices, and that means right now: no wounded, nutty or broken-winged men, no alcoholics or drug addicts, need apply—unless you're starting a rock band. No abusive, rude jerks who are nice one minute and mean the next, and then come crawling back in a spiral of guilt. These guys are not likely to get better, and if they do, it needs to be with professional help and not on your watch.

The good news is that there are enough people out there, enough fish in the sea, who don't have qualities that violate your core value system, so you don't have to take the guy who does. It's the most obvious rule in the world: Don't pick the one who is broken. It's like buying a car. If two cars are sitting there, and one has been wrecked while the other doesn't have a scratch on it, heck, even Lassie knows to pick the one that isn't damaged.

So besides the obvious problems that we just discussed, what are your personal deal breakers? If you are seriously religious and marrying someone outside your religion is something you can't deal with, just don't go down that aisle. If caring for your family and spending time with them is a big part of your life, but he prefers to spend time alone with you, that's a family feud waiting to explode. Nine out of ten times relationships like this end in heartbreak. If you are looking for meaningful eye contact, but he'd rather stare at his reflection in the mirror hanging over your head, then you may have a narcissist on your hands. If you detect even a hint of volatility, make a mental note. Do bar fights tend to follow him around? Does he have a hard time controlling his temper? I've often said the best predictor of future behavior is relevant past behavior. So look at the guy's history.

Do not think that you are such a potent female force that you are the one who can tame the beast. If he has been married three or four times, has had four affairs (that you know about), can't hold a job and is financially irresponsible, then he needs a tranquilizer gun, not a girlfriend. He may be cute and charming, but if he drinks, fights and gambles, then keep walking. I know that sounds so obvious I shouldn't be wasting time on it, but we both know people, maybe even you, who just don't seem to be able to steer clear. There are too many fish in the sea for you to pick one who has core compromising values, traits or characteristics. We will get a *suitable* fish in your boat—and once he's in there, you can gut him, clean him and fry him up anyway you want. Just kidding of course, but you are going to have options!

Now I've gone through and given you a short list of deal breakers worth considering, and you may have others. Once those are identified they become stop signs. Put them on your "eject" list and just don't go there.

What Not to Think

"I need to marry someone who my parents will love."

Look, I know it's hard to ignore what our parents, friends and society in general say we should want. Still, you simply cannot pick your partner according to others' expectations. While the opinions of the outside world can factor into your decision, you have got to be clear on and true to what *you* want.

Michael, my friend of twenty years, will tell you to this day that he married his wife because he had a terrible bad-boy reputation in their small town and he wanted to redeem himself by being with a Goody Two-Shoes who all the mothers just loved. She was Suzy Q sweetheart, the dream daughter and daughter-in-law. Marrying her made him respectable, or so he thought. It thrilled his parents. It was exactly what they wanted him to do. He even thought of himself as more virtuous because he married the good girl. But guess what—he's been miserable for twenty-five years now because he doesn't love her. He never did. Ever since they married, he's cheated on her left and right and occasionally sideways. He's always remained a bad boy to the core. He lacks certain traits and characteristics—that should have been a deal breaker for her, but she was tired of being the good girl and she wanted to walk on the wild side, so they both used each other to externally validate themselves. You don't want to do that. You have to decide what **you** truly want.

I'm not going to preach at you about what you should or shouldn't want (well, maybe a little preaching), but right or wrong, you have got to identify the traits and characteristics that work for you. I want you to do this as selfishly as possible, with no concern for anyone but yourself, so we can learn about your needs. Later, we will review your list to see if it is also healthy for you and good for you, but I want to make sure that the answers you give in the next part of the book describe what you want and not what you've been told you want or what you think you should want. This is a time to step up and look out for number one.

Now does that mean I want you to turn a deaf ear to your loved ones? Absolutely not. (Well, maybe.) Weigh their input carefully and decide how it squares with what you want and need. Then make your own decisions.

The Experience of You

I want you to assume for a moment that you have found somebody who rings your bell, lights your fire and gets your motor running—all at the same time. Let's just assume you've found him and he is totally a willing spirit. Tell me how you feel, knowing that this person is head-over-heels in love with you?

Are you feeling a sense of belonging? A sense of acceptance? Are you feeling lucky, blessed and proud of yourself and of your partner? Do you feel peace, joy, security? Do you feel you have finally found your place in this world through this person with whom you are going to share you life?

That is what you really want—those feelings and *not* the character of him are your real goal. So why are we about to go through the process of developing the Character of Him? Because those are the traits and qualities likely to create this feeling we have just described. So while it's important that you have a wish list, it's equally important to remember that you're actually looking for the character that will give you the feeling. And let me tell you, once you find that feeling, you will not care what wrapper it comes in.

For instance—and I can say this with almost 100 percent certainty—hardly any tall women grow up dreaming of marrying a guy who's barely tall enough to go on all the rides at an amusement park or needs a stepladder to change a lightbulb on a desk lamp. In fact, the first thing that most of the single tall women I know ask when considering a blind date is, "How tall is he?" But as far as tall married women go, their husbands come in a variety of sizes. And believe me, the tall girls who married short guys aren't sitting around cursing their fate. Far from it.

Finding true love is as much about you as your partner. Ask yourself: What do you want? "A best friend who makes you happy," "Someone you cannot live without," "A person with whom you want to share" . . . Notice that there's a lot of "you" in there because true love, whether you feel it or not, is up to you. It really is a choice.

And I don't want to make this too clinical, because I know there is some chemistry involved and lightning strikes and all that. I get that. I really do. But on the other hand, a lot of it is a mind-set in which you decide, "You know what? I'm going to bloom where I'm planted. This is where I am, so I'm going to commit to this and I'm going to do it."

And don't let yourself be seduced by his good looks; he has to make you feel the way you want to feel. Physical attributes that seem so important in the beginning become superficial. Height, weight, hair color, job and all those sorts of things that may have attracted you to him initially and made your chest swell with pride when you walk into a party together will be at the bottom of the list describing the Character of Him. That's because what you are looking for is the experience of you and not the Character of Him. And the things that will create this for you will be his values, personality style and interaction style, and the way he helps you to feel.

We will identify the Character of Him to give you some guidelines. But whether he's short, tall, quiet, spontaneous or laid back, it all comes down to what you feel when you are around him. Is your feeling going to be enough? "Well, geez," you say, "I feel that way with this alcoholic over here." You may feel that way now, it may ring your bell today, but it won't in the long term, and that is why you will need the guidelines we identify in this chapter.

The 80 Percent Solution

Let me give you a word of caution: If you think you have met Mr. Perfect, then you need to slap yourself in the face or take a cold shower, because you are mesmerized. The 100 percent candidate doesn't exist. That's right; the perfect fit is a myth right up there with painless dentistry and painless waxing. If you really believe there's a perfect fit, then you're probably still checking your messages for that guy you met at a club last year who promised he'd call. If you think you've found the perfect man, don't shout it from the rooftops. Go home, settle down and take it as a sign that love is blind and you are kidding yourself.

What I'm telling you is that instead of wasting time searching for an exact match, look for the guy who is free of the deal breakers and has 80 percent of what you do want in a partner. The other 20 percent you can grow. If the guy has 80 percent of what you want and potential to grow the extra 20 percent, you need to bag that boy up because he is good to go. Do not walk past him while you're looking for Mr. 100 Percent, because somebody else is going to marry Mr. 80 Percent and you are going to be standing there 60 percent sad and 40 percent frustrated.

I've counseled many couples and I've been friends with many couples and I will tell you that in all my years as a friend, therapist and human being interacting in the world, I have yet to run across the "perfect couple." That perfect couple is a myth, so do not waste your time trying to become the first. Am I telling you to compromise? Yes, of course I am. Life is a compromise. Relationships are a compromise. Does that mean you should give up on the 20 percent you don't like? No way. You work on it. And if all you ever get is 80 percent of that missing 20 percent, take my word, you are going to be married and happy for a long time.

Ultimately it comes down to the difference between the people who are serious about commitment and the people who are out chasing a fantasy—the former will gladly overlook the imperfections of an 80 percent partner for the time being, whereas the latter will keep on searching until they figure out that a 100 percent match is about as real as a hundred-dollar Rolex.

Husbands Unlimited

Since you're two chapters into this book, I figure that you mean business and I want to give you the tools you need to help you find your partner with minimum trial and error. Champions have a technique called visualization, whereby they actually see and feel what it is like to win before they've even started the game. You've already described what it would feel like to have what you want in the section of this chapter headed "The Experience of You." Now, we are going to envision the person who is going to make you feel all those wonderful, joyous emotions that will come with being part of a couple.

Imagine that we are making a movie of your life. Your job is to write a wonderful script about how you want your story to unfold, particularly your romantic story line. The first thing you'll have to do is describe your leading man, a.k.a. your future husband. I want you to be extremely specific when envisioning this man. To do that, you may need to think about the kinds of male characters you've seen in your life. Let's take some archetypal movie roles just as examples (these are neither real people nor good "yardsticks," but I use them as examples because we both know them): Tom Hanks is your sensitive dream guy in *Sleepless in Seattle*. He is a best friend, a father, a nurturer. He's funny and dry—the kind of guy who can fit in with any group. On the other end of the spectrum is Richard Gere in *Pretty Woman*. He plays a strong business tycoon—rich, powerful and commanding. He is generous and stable, cultured and sophisticated—a man who comes with a lifestyle. Then you have your passionate and emotionally expressive type in *Moonstruck*: Nicholas Cage. This guy is the essence of heat and chemistry. When he wants you, you know it, and neither rain, nor snow, nor hail nor sleet will stop him from going after you. The list goes on, but the characters are clear as day, and if you recognize them you know they had specific characteristics that went far beyond the brief description above.

That's how precise I want you to be when visualizing your future husband. You've got to think about what you want mentally, physically, emotionally, occupationally, socially, intellectually—all the things that make you say, "Hmmm, now there's a guy I wouldn't mind spending my life with." If you're going around saying, "I'll know it when I see it," I have news for you: The only thing you're going to see is everyone else meeting the right guy. So let's not waste another minute. Let's figure out what kind of guy you want right here and now.

Go through the following five lists and circle everything that you can imagine as a desirable trait in your special someone. Don't worry if your wish list seems too long. Circle as many items in each category as you desire. Think about you, your life and your potential targets as you go. Which qualities would get you all hot and bothered? Which ones will make your life easier? And which ones have you been looking for all along?

Now, it's perfectly okay to dream a little. I'm not saying that you are going to get all these things or that it's even reasonable to expect all these things, but let's start out with a full plate. Then we will see what you are willing to compromise on. What we are describing now is the guy who will ring your bell and light you up like a Christmas tree—beginning with the obvious:

1 **Personality:** Are you looking for an extrovert or a quiet guy? Do you want someone with a well-developed sense of humor, or are you tired of jokesters and want somebody who has a serious approach to life? Do you want someone emotionally expressive or a strong silent type? A leader or a follower? For instance, when a crisis strikes, do you want a guy who stands up and says, "The first thing we've got to do is get some duct tape and a flashlight"—or someone who says, "Now what are we going to do, hon?" Are you a free spirit who couldn't imagine being with someone who wants to make plans, or do you enjoy structure and need a guy who wouldn't mind scheduling every last hour of his week?

Your preferences here should be made with full consideration of what would complement or compensate for your personality. Some things you might prefer simply because they sound like admirable qualities, and that's fine, but take time to think about what characteristics would have the best long-term fit with who you truly are. You get the picture. Now circle the descriptions that are important to you:

- Funny—Makes me laugh out loud even when I'm having a bad day, which I haven't done since I saw the last Adam Sandler movie. Plus, I tend to be too serious and want to lighten up some.
- Serious—Isn't afraid to think or talk about the deeper issues in life. Seriousness is important to me because I detest superficiality and need someone to resonate with me mentally and emotionally. The class clown is the last person I need to be with.
- Leader—Knows how to take

charge both at home and at work, so I feel safe knowing that if things get out of control, he can step in and make them right.

- Supportive—Boosts my ego with plenty of praise and stands behind me no matter what. This is important because while I like to run things, I don't see myself as a Lone Ranger.
- Intellectual—Can participate in more esoteric discussions with me and our friends. This is important because I like to learn new things from my partner.
- Emotional—Feels deeply and can relate to me on more than an intellectual level. This is important because I have an active emotional life and I need someone who understands this side of me.
- Street-smart—Has great social skills and is a real survivor. He will make it in any circumstances. I need this either because I can be naive sometimes and I like to have someone around who knows the score, or just because I get how it

all works and don't want to spend my time teaching some guy who doesn't.

- Honest—Doesn't play games, but is candid and forthright with me, even when it's not easy—such as when he tells me I have food in my teeth and have had for days.
- Sensual—Brings out the sexual vixen in me. I need this because I am usually pretty calm in the sexual realm and need someone to stir up that side of me, or because I am so sensual that I tend to overpower partners who aren't.
- Motivated—Driven to succeed in every aspect of his life. This is important because I want to live like a queen and my kids to live like princes, not paupers.
- Stable—Lets me feel safe and comfortable because he is so solid. This is important because I am a free spirit and I need someone to be the ground beneath my feet, or because I work hard to be reliable and can't stand people who don't reciprocate.

- Carefree—Helps me escape from all my stress with his easygoing, go-with-the-flow attitude. This is great because life is too short to worry all the time.
- Spontaneous—Can live on the edge, pick up and go on the spur of the moment. This is important to me because I think too much planning takes all the fun out of having a good time.
- Unpredictable—Keeps me on my toes so that I am never bored. This is important because although I am quite structured, the thing I hate most in the world is getting stuck in a rut.
- Organized—Takes care of things like bills and makes sure everything that needs to get done does. This is great because I can actually be a little scatterbrained sometimes.
- Responsible—Can be relied upon to do what he says he will do. This is important because I need someone who can be my equal

partner when it comes to doing the stuff that's not fun as well as the stuff that is.

- Dangerous—Gives me intense emotions, huge ups and downs, and makes me feel that I'm really alive. This is important to me because I don't feel I've lived enough or because I'm bored to death any other way.
- Independent—Likes to spend a lot of time apart and allows me to do the same. He never makes me feel any pressure or makes me feel that I'm responsible for his emotions. This is great because nothing turns me off faster than pressure.
- Dependent—I feel certain that he'll never leave me, because he would be lost without me. That's important because I don't handle emotional pain well alone.
- Talkative—Keeps me entertained into the wee hours with great conversations. That's important to me because I also have lots to say.
- Confident—Believes in himself, and makes me believe in him. This

quality makes me feel good about my place in the world and secure in my future.

- Wise—Thinks before he acts because he has learned from his experience. This is important to me because I sometimes need guidance and would love to have a partner who can give me some real advice.
- Disciplined—Strong enough to structure his life and follow his own rules. This is important because I can always trust him to follow through on what he promises.

2 **Social skills:** Are you looking for someone who likes to go, do, be involved and have a social calendar that's bursting at the seams? Or would you prefer a homebody? Do you like the type who is socially conscious and politically motivated? Or are you partial to a guy whose sense of community comes from a strong sense of family? Do you want someone who likes to throw parties in your home, prefers to

be invited to others' homes or would choose a night by the warm glow of his computer screen over a party any day of the week?

Take some time to consider what would make you feel most comfortable or what you could easily get used to and circle those descriptions below:

- ♥ Corporate entertainer—He always has business associates to entertain.
- ♥ Political crusader—I'm not sure if he'd rather talk politics or have sex. Or have sex while talking politics.
- ♥ Family guy—Every night is family night: Scrabble, Monopoly, Twister. . . . He never gets tired of togetherness.
- ♥ Homebody—Would rather stay in his boxers and watch TV than go to all the trouble of going out.
- ♥ Late-night raver—Will dance the night away and then somehow still make it to work in the morning.
- ♥ Night crawler—Cannot stay in for

the life of him. Must be out and about all the time.

- Networker—Goes to lots of industry parties and events to rub elbows and distribute his card.
- Philanthropist, benefitgoer—Life is just one gala after another.
- Sports enthusiast—If there's a game on, you know where to find him: at some bar with big-screen TVs and sawdust on the floor.
- Jet-setter—He's a regular saint . . . as in he skis in Saint Moritz, summers in Saint-Tropez and winters in Saint Bart's.
- Part-time socializer—Likes to stay in, but will go out once in a while to have dinner with friends.
- Couple-crazy—Life for him is like one long "happy couple" montage from the movies. He wants to do everything with me and me alone.
- Dinner party thrower—His home is the place for food and fun.
- Dinner party goer—He is often invited to his friends' houses for parties.
- Dinner party avoider—He hates

parties and doesn't like to make the effort to maintain friendships.

- Nature lover (hiking and camping groups)—Card-carrying member of the Sierra Club. An Eagle Scout who likes getaways to national parks.
- Athlete—Big-time runner, Ironman triathlete, mountain climber and cross-country cyclist. This guy's life revolves around athleticism and peak performance.
- Good provider—We always have our material needs met.
- Good dad and husband—Dinner with the family after work, fun time with the kids on the weekends, and one night a week we go out, just the two of us.

3. **Relational style:** This is about how you want your dream guy to relate to you. Are you interested in somebody who wants you to be his everything and includes you in all the plans he makes? Or would you prefer a separate and private life and don't even mind a separate vacation now and

again? Do you want a romantic who says and does stereotypically romantic things? Because, let me tell you, if you need a love letter a week and you marry a guy who just doesn't have it in him, then you could be in for years of disappointment. The same goes for parenting styles. Do you prefer a guy who will pull his own weight in that department, or hand over the child rearing to you?

And what about the subject of money? Where does Mr. Wonderful stand on the role of finances in a relationship? Does he believe that it's a fiscal partnership, meaning it's "our" money and we will confer on all decisions, or does he prefer to take on the burden of responsibility for the financial planning? Do you want a guy who needs a nice house, a three-car garage, a souped-up stereo system, the latest TV, updated kitchen appliances, the works, or someone who doesn't put too much stock in material trappings?

Then you've got your sexual issues.

Do you want someone who is highly charged, or is once a month just fine by you? Are you a sexual vixen or traditional? You've got to know what you want in this regard. If you two are compatible in the sexual department, you will find an extra element of chemistry, heat and intensity in your relationship.

Take some time to think about the way your dream man would handle your relationship and then circle the descriptions that come to mind:

- Emotionally expressive. Articulates his feelings.
- Affectionate. Shows emotion through hugs and kisses.
- Romantic in all the ways Hallmark would expect.
- Actively involved parenting style.
- In control of finances.
- Willing to share responsibility for money.
- Highly sexual.
- Not that sexual.
- Aloof and doesn't need or give much attention.

- Compassionate but remains level-headed.
- Money-motivated and a go-getter who must have all the creature comforts.
- A bohemian free spirit who doesn't need many creature comforts.
- Someone who stubbornly demands to get his way.
- Open to compromise.
- Inseparable from you.
- In need of a lot of personal space.

4 **Spiritual compatibility:** Whether you are religious or not, the fact is that in a perfect world you would probably like your partner to agree with your view on this. Or not. Maybe you'd rather have a home with divergent perspectives. Whatever your position, again, it's best to know what you want going in. Spiritual beliefs are deeply ingrained during our upbringing, and the chance that someone will veer from a firmly held belief system is not great. Certainly, people are often born again, but if you're a faithful

Christian, maybe you shouldn't marry an atheist and pray for a miracle for the rest of your life. That is the definition of frustration.

Look over the following list and check off whichever approach to spirituality works for you.

- ♥ He is very observant of the same religion as you.
- ♥ He is somewhat observant of the same religion as you.
- ♥ He is not at all observant, but comes from the same religious background as you.
- ♥ He is not at all religious but believes in a higher power.
- ♥ He doesn't believe in a higher power at all.
- ♥ It doesn't matter what he believes as long as he is open-minded and respectful of your beliefs.

♡5 **Physical characteristics:** Now let's decide what you'd like Mr. Amazing to look like. Does he need to be a big man? Or maybe you're petite and you want a smaller guy? Is he athletic?

Does he need to have hair? (Watch it!) If so, do you like brown, blond or red hair? Sure, this may seem superficial; and, yeah, you may well be thinking, "Who cares? As long as he has all the other things I want?" I get it, but humor me. It's definitely not the only thing—it's not even an important thing—but it's part of the formula you get. So go ahead, fill in or circle what you'd want if you had your druthers.

- Hair color, hair style.
- Eye color.
- Age.
- Height.
- Body type: athletic, skinny, muscular, average size.
- Nice voice.

That was the fun part. You now have your 80 percent guy—at least on paper. Now comes the hard part. Whenever you merge two lives, there is always going to be some pain of adjustment. You have to be willing to sacrifice some of your time, space, money, effort and freedom—and you certainly have to be willing to compromise on some of what you want.

Now that you're through circling your wants, go back over your choices and cross off all the luxury items you can do without. And by that, I mean anything that can fall into the 20 percent of the 80-20 formula. What remains is your standard. The guy who fills this bill may not ring your bell right away, but if you let him lure you away from your Tivo, you may just wind up having a great time.

Get Serious

Now look over your list of needs one more time. Is it still too long? Is everything a must-have? Have you left no room for compromise? Are you limiting yourself with your high standards? Take some time to consider your choices in the past. Or, if you have to, consider the cell phone that just isn't ringing these days. What are the problems? If your list is as long as my arm, I know why no men are calling—you're more exclusive than the VIP room at the *Vanity Fair* Oscar party!

This is the time to put on some binoculars and look a little deeper into the field of candidates. Say you need a car. You want power seats but you've got to have air conditioning. Now suppose you can't afford both. Are you going to spend the rest of your days walking to work or are you going to trim your list? So let's say you meet a guy who has the honesty and the ambition. Maybe you can learn to live without the sense of humor.

If all the wrong men are calling you, then you've got the opposite problem. You're not being discriminating enough. Mass marketing can be very lucrative—if you've come up with a great new product for storing leftovers. But if you're marketing your much sought-after companionship, it could be that you are selling yourself short. You will be flooded with requests and have no smart way to pick and choose. I know one young woman who spends about two nights a month at home. I am not kidding you. She is out all the time, either with her friends or with some guy. But one of the producers I work with spends time with her, and the way she tells it, it's a pretty sorry sight. The girl will go out with anyone who asks. Heck, even fast-food restaurants don't let everyone in. These two women have hit the town together, and the producer tells me, "You wouldn't believe the loser that was hitting on Marisol last night. But get this—she actually gave him her number. Her real number." The girl has no filter. She will go out with anybody who asks. She's almost thirty years old, but she's still as desperate for attention as a five-year-old.

So look at your list. Is it, in fact, too short? Maybe you've been an equal-opportunity dater to a fault. And maybe by now, you're starting to believe that all men are losers because you meet so many inappropriate ones. If you marked less than five qualities on that wish list, you need to put up some fences around yourself, lady. You may be easier to get into than a community college. Have some boundaries. Get to know your real tastes. And don't simply listen to the you who can't stand to be alone. Don't be the girl who would rather have a date, any date, than spend an evening with a hot bath and a good book. When you do that, you inadvertently cause yourself to be alone—or at least in company with the wrong people, and that can be a very lonely place.

Bad-Boy Bait

You know as well as I do that when that biological clock starts sounding like the beginning of *60 Minutes* and you've started going to your friend's *second* weddings, it's all too easy to panic. You get desperate and think, "Who's got time for standards? I'll just be anybody's dog who will hunt with me—anybody who will have me will do, or anybody who'll do me I'll have!" You are not going to do that. That's why we just spent so much time identifying the traits and characteristics you want.

If you don't believe you're worthy of getting what you want, you can turn even an altar boy into a bad boy. We show people how to treat us, so if your cell phone is blowing up with booty calls from players, take a good hard look at how you perceive yourself and answer the following questions:

1. *Would I prefer more respectful treatment from guys?*
2. *Do I go along with what others want more often than not?*
3. *Do I put the feelings of others above my own?*
4. *Do I often ignore, deny or overlook my true feelings?*
5. *Am I afraid that if I don't do what others want, they will leave?*

If you answered "yes" to just one or two of the above questions, you can relax, because you are not looking for a bad boy. What you are doing, however, is asking these boys to treat you badly. In Chapters 3 and 4, I will show you how to stop projecting your doubts into the world and start sending the message that you deserve respect.

Now that we've gone through what you want in a guy and what you know you will not tolerate, you've got some idea of your target. More important, however, you've realized that you cannot get excited about a résumé or a written-out list of qualities. What gets you going is the thought of a partnership with someone you respect and want to spend time with, and the sense of belonging and happiness that this guy provides.

The warm, fuzzy experience of being part of a couple—that right there is your target. Not some guy who fits the suit and all your criteria. Guys who fit the suit are a dime a dozen—it's the guys who help you to feel, the ones who give you the experience you want, who take time to find. But now that you know what you're after, you'll find that the search will be a lot easier.

3

The Character of You

But the most exciting, challenging and significant relationship of all is the one you have with yourself. And if you find someone to love the you you love, well, that's just fabulous.

CARRIE BRADSHAW, *SEX AND THE CITY*

If you're like the thousands of women I've talked to, you're probably thinking there are millions of hot, young, single girls and all the good guys are taken or gay—or maybe even both. You're doing everything in your power to keep up. Hundred-dollar haircuts? Check. Trips to all the right vacation spots? Double check. A membership at the gym? Hanging out at the target-rich environments otherwise known as "trendy nightclubs" or "new restaurant bars"? Check, check, check. And still, you feel as though you're wearing yourself out, running on a treadmill and getting nowhere fast and sweating in the process. You're sitting around scratching your head and wondering, "What's wrong with me? Why her and not me? What am I—some kind of dog biscuit? Why can't I seem to get a guy to save my life while that girl who is unkempt, sloppy, smokes and has five piercings in her lip is walking hand in hand with what looks like Jude Law's younger brother! Or some guy who may not look like much, but who seems pretty cool."

I don't know how to answer that specific question, because I don't know you. Maybe there *is* something people perceive as wrong. Maybe they think you look, act or smell funny, I don't know, but I'm betting it's none of those three things. I'm not going to kid you: It's a dog-eat-dog dating world out there, and if you want to win and have the relationship that you want you're going to have to raise your game. And yes, in my opinion, at least at this level and stage, it is "a game." I know, I know, I can hear some of you with all the progressiveness of Aunt Bee saying, "Well, Andy, I don't think finding a life partner to enter into the sanctity of marriage is any kind of a game. So there." All I can tell you is that you aren't walking down the aisle just yet, so lighten up about 1,000 percent and have some fun!

The social marketplace is highly competitive, and men and women have been "playing the game" and "doing the dance" for centuries. It doesn't cheapen the process if you play with integrity and are who you are. First and foremost, you have to know yourself and then commit to who that is.

So how are you going to go from sitting on the sidelines and watching other people score to taking the ball to the hoop yourself? How are you going to jump off the endless dating merry-go-round, where it's one cool jerk after another, and not one of them can commit to a hairstyle, much less to a relationship with you? Seriously, what are you going to do—short of moving to Alaska, joining a fraternity or getting a job on the floor of the stock exchange where the odds are ten to one in your favor?

The first thing I'm going to tell you is that you're probably right: Carole in accounting may not be funnier or prettier or cooler than you. The reason you've spent the last four

Friday nights watching TV with your cat while her weekend nights are booked months in advance is that she is better—better at the game. I've said it a million times, "Either you get it or you don't." What you need to get is what this chapter is all about—how to identify the best-quality Character of You. That means being honest with yourself about your strengths and weaknesses, which isn't always easy. It can be painful to admit that you may sometimes be shy or controlling, or whatever your weaknesses may be, but knowing and accepting them gives you a confidence that can't be faked. This awareness also allows you to understand how those traits may turn people off, in the short or long term, and how you can rein them in so they don't interfere with your relationships.

Once you've identified and embraced every part of the Character of You, you can put whichever traits you wish out into the world as a defined product. Take me, for example. When you tune in to the *Dr. Phil* show, buy a Dr. Phil book or go to a Dr. Phil speech, you know what you are going to get because it is a defined product. It is going to be a straightforward, no-nonsense, in-your-face representation of reality. That is the defined product that is Dr. Phil. But that is not a full representation of my Character of You. There is so much more, like what I am like as a husband, a father, a member of my church community; what I personally believe and value; my life story—you don't get to see all that in every situation. But whatever particular setting you encounter me in, what you do get to see is a true subset of my Character of You. It's authentic, it's genuine, it's me, but it is what I choose to put out that is appropriate to that situation.

The Character of You is the broad and all-encompassing definition of who you are from the inside out, while the defined product is whatever side you choose to exhibit in a given social situation. Now make no mistake: After you've decided that this is the horse you are going to ride through the race called life, your entire experience in the social, dating and creating-a-relationship arena will change forever.

I'll say it again because it bears repeating: **The first person you have to sell yourself to is you.** That is the crucial first step to identifying the Character of You. I call it defining your personal truth—it's what you say to yourself when no one else is looking. If you're telling everyone that you're the greatest thing since the iPod, but deep down inside you believe you are an eight-track player or the "chubby girl" who couldn't catch a man with a net and a pack of hunting dogs, then you're heading for more nights alone than a cloistered nun. You will generate the results that correspond to your personal truth.

I mean it. I don't care how polished your presentation is or how ironclad your argument; if you have a crummy personal truth, you can look like Miss Universe for all I care. If underneath it all, you believe you're living a big lie because you're really just an unlovable outsider who is destined to wander the planet alone, people will sense it in a heartbeat and run the other way. They will figure, "Hey, she knows herself better than anyone else, and if she thinks she's worthless, who am I to argue? See ya!" Or maybe you'll find some loser who doesn't care who he's with or who you are, just so long as he's got somebody—anybody. That's not what you want either. You deserve better. Trust me—there's a world of difference between being with the one and being with someone. If you're out there acting as if you'll take whatever you can get because beggars can't be choosers, you're destined to wind up with the scraps.

When your personal truth is negative and riddled with doubts, distortions and shame, you scream that message to the world in a million and one nonverbal ways. What you believe is your "real deal" reflects itself in your body language, your facial expressions and your actions, which all conspire to contradict every word you say and the impression you strive to make.

Oh, I get it all right. You have a history that maybe you're not proud of. Maybe you've slept with enough guys to make up two football teams—including the practice squads. Maybe you've been dumped or left standing at the altar. The point is that all this stuff is in the past and you can't do anything to change it. What you can do is start spending 5 percent of your time trying to figure out whether you screwed up or got a raw deal, and 95 percent of your time figuring out what you're going to do about it.

Now, it's possible that you have some deeply entrenched scarring in your life such as molestation or abuse. If these things have happened to you, your suffering is very real and understandable. A damaged self-image, compromised self-worth and negative self-truth are all to be expected. Do not for one second trivialize those experiences by telling yourself that you've got to gut up and get over it. Those experiences can cause you to devalue yourself. They can lead to decades of believing that you are damaged goods who no one would want for any reason other than sexual gratification. While it is wrong thinking, it is understandable. You will probably need to get professional help to overcome that—and not because you need it, but because you deserve it. Whether you ever form a relationship with someone else or not, the most important relationship you will ever have is the one with yourself. So get help, if not for the sake of creating a healthy relationship, then for the sake of creating your own peace and joy in this life.

Getting your personal truth straightened out is the first step to identifying the Character of You. Everything about your message, everything about your aura, everything about you will change. If you are not sure about the contents of your personal truth, now is the time to ask yourself some hard questions:

1. *Do I feel that I have to disguise myself?*
2. *Do I live with shame?*
3. *Do I live with guilt?*
4. *Do I believe that I lack intelligence?*
5. *Is there something fundamentally wrong with me?*
6. *Do I lack confidence?*
7. *Do I think my ______ (best friend, sister, etc.) is somehow better than I am?*
8. *Do I feel like a fraud?*
9. *Do I think I am a second-class citizen?*
10. *Do I feel unworthy of love?*

11. *Do I often feel I have no control over my life and behavior?*
12. *Am I damaged goods—have I been dumped so many times that there has got to be something wrong with me?*
13. *Do I feel that I am not as smart, sharp or interesting as other people?*
14. *Do I believe that I am not going to find happiness?*
15. *Do I say to myself that I'm not worthy?*
16. *Do I feel that I am masquerading and just one step ahead of being found out?*
17. *Do I believe that I'm totally clueless in comparison with my peers?*
18. *Do I play the game constantly afraid of being hurt and humiliated?*

I have just taken you through a structured examination of possible negative content in your personal truth. The first thing that should go on your to-do list is to eliminate, heal, change, do whatever you have to do so that it no longer has an impact on you. Hopefully, much of or most of your personal truth is positive. The majority of people have a combo deal.

The reason we are doing this inventory of negative personal truths is that we all generate the results we feel we deserve. So if you can eliminate, minimize and manage the negatives, you will be able to maximize the positives and present the results that are consistent with someone who has positive self-worth. In other words, if you don't like you, you will not get anyone else to like you. If you love you, then other people will love you. If you believe that you deserve the best relationship, you will attract a healthy, positive, fulfilling relationship into your life.

It's as simple as your personal truth saying, "I am a quality person and so I should be treated in a quality fashion." So when some jerk rolls up, slaps you on the butt and says, "Hey, baby, you want to take a tumble?" you can say, "Wait a minute. You don't talk to me that way, jerk. I deserve better treatment than that. You address me as a lady with dignity and respect or you don't address me at all." But if you are sitting there thinking, "Geez, I will take what I get because nobody wants me," and somebody slaps you on the butt, you may think, "Well, at least I'm getting groped and it's better than being alone." Then you're getting what you expect. You should be telling yourself, "I deserve somebody to spend time with me, share experiences with me and get to know me. Not grab my ass." If your personal truth is negative, you will settle for being groped. If it is positive, you won't.

That is why I do not want the negative voices in your head screaming louder than the positive voices. If any of the answers to the above questions is yes, roll up your sleeves and prepare to do some real work. To truly sell yourself on you, you'll have to change each one of those self-destructive answers and the perceptions that led you to them into positive, constructive thoughts. Once you have sold yourself on you, you'll realize that you don't need a man in your life to be whole. And that's getting your head in the game—coming at it with the mind-set of a winner, not a loser. Because if you're telling yourself that you had better find a partner fast or you'll just curl up and die, then you are playing with sweaty palms, running scared, coming off desperate and turning guys off—and guys sense desperation the way a dog senses an earthquake;

and when they do, they take off and never look back. You've been doing fine on your own all these years, so just go for it. It's not so frightening to go out and show the world who you are.

The Character of You Dying to Get Out

Who are you? Don't just gloss over this question. This part is critical to defining the Character of You, so take it seriously. Give it some real thought and answer, who are you? Now write it down:

I am ______________________________

If you said a teacher, a student, a daughter and sister, a Christian or a single white female, try again. Who are you?

I am ______________________________

Annoying, isn't it? "Who are you?" is a question that leads to another question: "What do you mean?" Do you want my name? My age? My religion? My gender? My occupation? My role in my family? Who

I am with my friends? The person I am with my business associates? So many of us despise this question. We don't like writing about ourselves, or talking about ourselves. We don't even like thinking about ourselves all that much. And that is a big problem if you're looking to make a love connection.

Getting noticed in the singles scene is all about getting in touch with your own unique character. That is your power, and nothing—I repeat, nothing—else will do. You have to know who you are and forget about everything else. When I do interviews, sometimes beamed via satellite to stations all over the country, I can wind up talking to dozens of anchorpeople in the space of one day. Sometimes it feels like speaking to the same person over and over. Sure, they have different names and come from different states, but they each have the same purchased smile, the same flawless hair and the same Rhonda Radio from Nowhere USA voice. No accent, no uniqueness, no distinctiveness. The ones I remember, the ones who really stick out, are the ones who have a little attitude, the spicy ones who are people first and anchors second. And it's not that they're surly or unfriendly, it's just that they're not desperately trying to erase their individuality to fit central casting's "reporter mold."

You have to be distinctive like this. You don't want to be any old face in the crowd. You may think all eyes go to the tall, skinny blondes when they come into the room, but don't they all kind of look alike? Be someone distinctive. I'm not saying you should try to appeal to everybody. There's no way you are out there trying to get everybody in your zip code to date you. That's easy, and so is the girl who does that—which is about the nicest thing you can say about her. We all know what we call that girl. You are just trying to find that one guy who has the Character of Him that fits with the Character of You.

Some of you are the Jennifer Aniston type: sweethearts with a charm and magnetism you can't help loving. Then you've got your Angelina Jolie sexpot types. Both women are highly successful, both are highly attractive, both would appeal to an awful lot of men—even to the same man . . . but these women are as different as day and night. They make an impression precisely because they are so distinct. And that's what you have to do—make an impression. Luckily, there are a lot of different ways to do this that don't involve dating Brad Pitt.

You can take your pick of ways to be a champ, but there's one sure way to be a chump—and that is to fade into the background. The worst thing that can happen is that you go to a party or a social event and the next day, a group of guys who were there are talking and not one of them could pick you out of a lineup! If not one of them can remember if you were the tall girl or the blond girl or the girl with the talking parrot on her shoulder simply because you failed to have an impact of any sort, then welcome to Singleville, population: You!

You want each one of those guys to have a very clear and distinct recollection of you. One may have liked you and another may not have cared for you at all, but—most important–both of them noticed you and have no problem recalling you and their experience of you. How do you make sure that this happens every time? Answer: You identify your unique Character of You and form a defined product that you show the world. Commit to it, maximize it, embrace it and love it. That is the horse that you are going to ride. Some people will like it and some won't, but if it is uniquely you and you commit to it, you are going to get someone else to commit to it as well.

This all starts by you accepting that you are who you are. But that doesn't mean you shouldn't improve yourself where and when you can. This is not an excuse to be lazy. If you are overweight, jack it up and get the extra pounds off—not only for the sake of your appearance, but for your health, energy, self-esteem and general attitude. Superficial? Maybe, but if you want to win, you're going to have to work at it and take your game to the next level. The difference between winners and losers is that winners do things losers do not want to do.

If your hair and clothes look right out of *I Love the 80s,* then change them! You don't want people to see you and think, "Oh, yeah. I'm old enough to remember when that was in style!" Look around, have some social sensitivity and clean up your act. Don't tell yourself that it's okay and that it shouldn't matter if it's not okay. It does matter. If some quality is changeable and worth changing, change it! A five-year-old knows you should change it. As for those qualities you can't change, like your height, your general intelligence, your upbringing and your background, it's time to accept it and don't look back.

Self-Love Boot Camp

If I've said it once, I've said it a thousand times: People trust authorities. Think of yourself as the authority on you—if you think you're damaged goods, the rest of us will just have to take your word for it. Men will follow your lead just as surely. If you take yourself for granted and underestimate yourself, you will get exactly the same reaction from men. They will barely remember your name as they're searching for their socks the next morning. If you think you're it, one of the most exciting women on the face of the planet, guess what your dates are likely to think?

It is a mistake to think that love just happens to us and that we cannot fall in love on purpose. Each and every single one of us who has ever felt love has created that feeling. The only problem is that some of us don't know how we did it. Follow these steps to simulate the feeling of falling in love—except this time, the object of your affection will be none other than you. It'll be fun and you won't even have to buy a new wardrobe to impress yourself.

1. *Take a profound interest in you: Remember how fascinating the life of your love interest once seemed? You were interested in him, so you were interested in what he was doing. To fall in love with yourself, you'll have to express the same level of interest in yourself, your life and everyone in it. What that means is:*

   a. *Taking stock of your past and creating a rich personal history,* filled with stories and anecdotes you don't mind sharing with others because you know they are fascinating.

b. Playing a more active role in social and family functions because you want to know all about the people who are so closely connected to you.

c. Becoming more engaged in your work and with your coworkers because that is where your love interest—you—spends the majority of her time.

2. Be your own best friend: If you want to see yourself clearly, just step into the shoes of your closest friends. What do they see when they look at you? Probably not the things you complain about, but all the things that keep them coming back for more of your company: Your easy laugh. Your compassionate ear. Your sound advice. Your fun-loving spirit. Get very clear on what it is about you that draws people in. Then spend your time contemplating that idyllic image.

3. Only have eyes for you: The grass is always greener on the other side, except when you are in love. When you are losing your head over Jim, you don't stop to think, "Gee, Jim is great, but I wish his name were George . . . Clooney." Instead, you believe you have found the best of all possible worlds because of the connection you've forged. That is how I want you to feel good about yourself. Connected. I want you to stop comparing yourself with the Miss Thangs with their flat bellies and endless legs, and start admiring yourself for your great smile, smooth skin and hopeful outlook.

In this chapter, we're going to begin improving your game so that one day, someone can look at you walking with your boyfriend or husband and say, "What does she have that I haven't got—I mean, besides that great guy on her arm?" When that happens, you can just smile and hand her your dog-eared copy of this book.

I'm betting that those girls you're "hating," the ones with the really decent boyfriends, the ones you're going to be like by the time we're through, either just got dumb lucky being in the right place at the right time or really did have something that you just don't have. That something is what I call a defined product and a strategy for exhibiting it to the world. Women who get what they want in life and love have figured out their own best and most powerful combination of traits, behaviors, physical attributes and personality characteristics that sets them distinctively apart from all the other women in the world. They've turned these into their defined product—and then they've worked it for all it's worth.

Think of a choir of beautiful voices, all great but none distinguishable from the others. Then a soloist steps up and that voice rises above the rest with angelic tones. That is what we have to do with you. You have to rise above the noise. You have to become the figure against the wallpaper of the world. You have to stand out against the background. And to do that, we will have to identify the characteristics that set you apart from the women around you and make you the soloist in the choir of your life.

Now you may be thinking, "Oh boy, we've hit a snag here because I'm just not that special. I just don't have those unique traits and characteristics." That's why I'm here—to tell you that this is not true. You may not appreciate your finest qualities right now, but we are going to find them before we go on to the next two chapters. Granted, the end result may not be what you had hoped for. It may not be everything that you would order up and plug into yourself if you were going down a cafeteria line—"I'll take one order of that shiny hair and a helping of charisma, please; and thank you very much!" You're not Ms. Potato Head, you can't stick on a new nose, ears and a mouth, and those who try end up looking more fake than a Halloween mask—and usually a heck of a lot scarier. But I promise you will find that what you do have is worthy of being loved and cared for by somebody that you love and care about. You just can't continue to be the best-kept secret in your life.

Men are not dating detectives. They are typically not out there consciously looking for a life partner with the same vigor that women have. They are not going to come into your life with the sole purpose of assessing whether or not you are "the one." They're not going to dig and root around looking for the traits, qualities and characteristics that are the best fit for their special someone. They may not even know what those traits, qualities and characteristics are. Men will spend endless time researching a new car or a boat or which big-screen TV has the best picture, but they just don't have that relationship-marriage "chip" in their brain at the same level women do, which we will talk about in Chapter 6. That means you are going to have to get their attention. Telling them what they think they want to hear is not the answer. Trying to guess what they think they want and fill that bill is not the answer. As you are about to find out, you are not for everybody. But you, and not some people-pleasing version of you, will be right for somebody.

If you wonder how it is that some people find the partner they are looking for and some don't, I can promise you that one of the big factors is that they have embraced their Character of You and defined that character's product. It's this clear and distinct product that caused somebody to be attracted to them. It was powerful because it was real; it was authentic, and it was accepted by them long before they decided to try and get it accepted by "him."

Everybody, including you, has a certain constellation of traits and characteristics that, once identified and displayed, creates a power you cannot begin to imagine. As I said, I don't want you to continue to be the best-kept secret in your life. I don't want you waiting for "dumb luck." I want you to make your own luck.

My wife, Robin, is in my view a crystal-clear example. I will admit that, at least in my opinion, she's got a big plus that a lot of people don't have. She is and always has been a smooth-running "ten." And I admit it was her looks that got my attention from minute one, but when I met her and started talking to her, I was mesmerized. She had a kind of assured attitude: "I am who I am, I know what I want and if you don't like it, someone else will." (I still think she was kind of bluffing and was crazy in love with me, but she will never 'fess up!) She was spunky, irreverent and a definite enigma. She wasn't Goody Two-Shoes and she certainly wasn't a "bad girl." She was, however, a distinctly spunky "double dog dare ya" sort of girl who was fun, unpredictable and had a great spirit of adventure. When it was time to let loose, she was definitely "Woohoo!" When it was time to be quiet, she was powerfully and magnetically connected. Never, never boring. That was her defined product. I know it was authentic because it felt authentic then, and thirty-plus years later it hasn't changed one whit. It sets her apart from everyone else. She didn't care if she had makeup on or whether her hair was perfectly groomed or sticking out in twenty-four directions—she was always the same sparkly, spunky Robin. You knew when you were with her you would never be bored. Before I knew it, I was working really hard to win her approval, a really good place for her to be in. I want exactly that for you.

I want you to be in the power position in your relationships so that you are the one pursued, rather than the pursuer. And trust me, that is what you need to go for. If you have to run him down like a hungry cheetah after a gazelle, you don't want him anyway. Relationships are tough enough when the two people are running toward each other; you don't need a relationship where he is squirming to get loose. You want to get his attention, get him to notice who you can be in his life and then let him be "Cheetah Boy." So you need an edge. That way, when you find the special guy and he finds you, he will wonder where you have been all his life.

You all know those girls who can come into a room and just own it. They may not be the prettiest ones in the crowd, they may not fit the media's image of what is conventionally attractive, they're probably not even the ones flashing the most skin, yet they always seem to be getting all the attention. Love 'em or hate 'em. But here's the key part: It's *confidence and self-acceptance* that are making them so radiant, and those come only once you've mastered the first rule of the game, which also happens to be the first rule of sales: If you're not sold on your product, you won't be able to sell anyone else on it either.

You have to get right with you first. And I don't mean just telling yourself a bunch of rah-rah positive thinking. I mean really discovering your best attributes, your most desirable traits, the actual characteristics that make you distinct. If you are sitting there saying, "Look, I know a funny girl or a good-looking girl when I see one, and I ain't it." That's okay. That must not be the Character of You and that's fine. I promise you, if fully embraced and presented to the world, whoever you are and whatever you have going are plenty good enough.

Most of us can pick ourselves apart. Look at me. I have a "bad hair day" every day! But so what? How many Hollywood stars have you looked at and said, "How in the world did that person ever get famous?" Case in point: Danny DeVito. The man is barely five feet tall, overweight and bald. If you are filling out résumés for leading men, I don't think you will see those traits on the short list. Yet he is a celebrity. Why? (1) He is talented, (2) he is likable and (3) he is distinctly different from anyone else.

If Danny had sat on the sidelines saying, "I have a face and body for radio," we wouldn't have been able to enjoy his screen presence.

"Yeah, but he's a guy," you say. "It's different for guys," right? Well, then, just look at a woman like Kathy Bates. She may not be conventionally Hollywood or exotically attractive, but yet she is such a charismatic and powerful person that you can't take your eyes off her! She is cute, funny and multitalented. So don't sell yourself short just because you don't meet the typical standard. You do not have to measure yourself by traditional, typical standards of what makes a person attractive and appealing.

Here's What I've Got Versus What He Wants

The common complaint I hear from men is that they're dating Stepford women. They go out on a date, and all they hear is, "Oh, yes, I completely agree." That is great at first. Why wouldn't you love someone who likes all your ideas, laughs at all your jokes, focuses solely on you and buys into everything you say? But one log won't burn.

If you are nothing more than a yes-girl there is no spark, no tension, no heat, no interplay. It's boring. You become totally predictable and never challenge him. You become an accessory.

I'm going to let you in on a little secret: men need to feel that they have worked for and earned something, or they will not value it. Easy come, easy go. If you give up too easily, you're not going to hold his interest. At first, being agreeable is all well and good, but eventually we want to know your genuine opinion, and if you don't have one, you are snooze city. A guy could pick up a coma patient and get the same thrill he has with you. All men want is a genuine opinion. It doesn't matter if the opinion is different or even shocking—as long as it's real and honest and doesn't involve human sacrifice, a guy is happy. He is entertained. He is interested. He is curious. He feels that he's getting to know you.

Seems simple, but the fact is that a large percentage of women would sooner shave their heads and join the Krishnas than express an honest opinion and run the risk of turning off their date. Some of you may be shaking your heads, thinking, "Oh no, that couldn't possibly apply to me." Well, I wouldn't bet on that. Since men have traditionally been the pursuers, women have been conditioned to look for signs of interest from men *before* beginning to assess their own feelings. It's the old attitude: "I'll ace the interview, get the job, then decide whether to take it"—great in business, terrible in dating. In fact, this is precisely the attitude that leads so many to turn against dating altogether because they can't face the prospect of another "job interview" date.

Trying to be all things to all people is at

the root of these lackluster dates and shallow conversations, and it is the single biggest mistake women make when they are dating.

Those of you still sitting here thinking, "Well, what if I just don't have any great characteristics?" are not off the hook either. Let me put it to you this way: What is the best of what you've got? I'm not saying that if you had your druthers, you'd pick those traits out of a catalog, but relatively speaking, given only what you have to work with, what are your long suits? Think of it this way. If we were lost in a forest and had to survive, the first thing I would ask is, What do we have? Do we have blankets, a compass, flares, matches, food, a tent? If I'm out there and I don't have a tent, I'm going to pull branches off trees and cover myself up so I don't get frostbite. Sure, I would rather have a tent and a Coleman lantern and a nice campfire, but I'm living in the real world, so I'm going to make the most of what I've got—two arms, two legs and a survival instinct that propels me to construct a makeshift shelter.

Some women are really good at this "use what the good lord gave you" approach.

Recently Robin and I were attending a function at a governor's mansion. Both of us were going to be making a speech in front of a distinguished black-tie crowd. But when she opened her suitcase, she realized that she had brought only one shoe. Then, in her haste to get dressed, she broke one of the spaghetti straps on her gown. So here we are: clock ticking, broken strap on gown and one shoe. Did she panic? No. Next thing I know, she comes out of the room looking like a million bucks. I have no idea how she did it, but she never missed a beat. You women know how to make the best of what you've got and you do it every day of your life. Think of every time you've ever done something like this, whether it was when you fixed that unraveled hem using a glue gun or created an entire lunch from what looked to anyone else to be an empty refrigerator. All of that was preparation for what we are talking about here, right now. All those experiences were just preparing you for this moment in time.

When it comes to defining yourself, there is a distinct difference between women who say, "Here's what I've got" and those who ask, "What do you want?" The former are defining themselves in terms of what they have to offer. The latter are trying to define themselves in terms of what they think people want—a recipe for disaster if I've ever heard one.

I'll tell you right now, you will not know what your defined product is until you've identified your strongest attributes, traits, assets and characteristics. So you need to take an inventory and then present your findings to the world, instead of going around lamely trying to be all things to all people. Chronic people pleasing either puts the kibosh on the relationship from the start because your potential partner senses your motives and gets bored, or it kills the relationship slowly, after you disappoint all the expectations you've set up. When Robin and I first started dating, I told her that I play tennis. When I asked her if she played tennis, she said, "Oh yeah." So I thought, "Oh, great, she looks great and a tennis player too." So we made arrangements to play, and the first thing she said to me when she got in the car was, "Okay, I give. I don't know how to play tennis." We both just about died laughing—and then I beat her in straight sets, or could have beaten her. She fessed up so quickly that I wasn't annoyed. I loved the attitude and honesty.

There is no surer way to fail than to sacrifice who you are for the sake of success, popularity or a relationship. Take me, for example. Growing up, I knew I was never going to be Robert Redford or Paul Newman. My nose was broken seven times and I started going bald at twenty-two. Model material I wasn't. But I *was* big, tall, athletic and fairly smart. So I became that tall guy with a great sense of humor. I was comfortable with that, so others were comfortable with me. Maybe you wouldn't fall in love with me at first sight, but give me a minute. I might sneak up on you if you are not careful.

Not much has changed since those days. I showed up in Hollywood, where everyone is under thirty, is tan and has great hair. Check the cover of this book if you need to refresh your memory, but that is not what I look like. A lot of people said, "Oh, you're fifty, you're balding and you have that distinctive Texas drawl; that's not going to work on TV." But I'll tell you right now that in a world where everyone is desperately trying to look like Johnny Depp, looking like yours truly can mean big success. The fact that I'm bald alone is enough to make me one of the most recognizable faces on TV. Yes, I'm middle-aged. Yes, I have a unique speech pattern. Yes, I'm not the handsomest devil to ever grace the silver screen. So what? If you're looking for eye candy, you've got hundreds of channels to choose from. Believe me, it's no accident that I'm doing a *talk show,* not a look-and-see show. You're not going to find me on the WB's new hot-guy drama. I do a *talk* show because *talking* is my long suit. So if you're looking for someone with something to say, I'm your guy.

Think Different

On the whole, people who have never taken the pains to identify their Character of You and define their product don't think all that highly of themselves. It's as if they're still the same vulnerable eighth-grader who got teased for a bad haircut or a funny pair of shoes. They want to blend in instead of stand out, because if they blend in, people won't notice them to make fun of them or criticize them. The essence of the defined-product strategy runs counter to that type of logic because it's all about getting noticed.

It's about not buying a Prada bag if you can't afford to pay the credit card bills. It's about not agreeing to go for sushi if you are not a fan of raw fish. It's about not saying that you're twenty-nine if you are really thirty-five. You don't have to be rich. You don't have to love sushi. You don't have to be young. You don't have to go along to get along. All you have to be is genuine. Trust me, there is someone out there who wants you precisely for who you are and what you have to offer. You just have to figure out what that is first.

4

Single—There Are No Accidents

I've been on so many blind dates,
I should get a free dog.
WENDY LIEBMAN

A few years ago, one of my producers, Kate, came into my office, plopped down in a chair and said, "What am I doing wrong? In my job, I have been exposed to some of the best life-changing advice ever, and yet I just can't make a long-term, committed relationship happen. When I was twenty-seven, I was thinking if the right guy crossed my path, I would definitely consider settling down. But cut to ten years and three failed engagements later, and I am starting to look at those I had tossed aside and peruse them for who would make the best sperm donor! I wouldn't say I'm beginning to panic, but how could ten years go by and I still haven't found the 'one'? What am I doing wrong?"

Well, I knew how hard Kate worked. The hours she put in at the office left precious little time for nurturing a relationship. So I asked her to list her priorities for me. Sure enough, like many unmarried thirty-seven-year-old women, she had marriage and children at the top of her list. Then, I asked her how many hours a week she devoted to this priority.

"Hmmm," she replied. "I guess, maybe about three or four hours."

That's barely enough time to go out on Saturday night with her friends or on a fix-up! Needless to say, the time she allotted to finding a life partner did not reflect the high priority she placed on accomplishing this goal. Once she put emphasis on making the time, things began to change and she is now happily married with two precious babies.

I frequently get asked by both men and women why I think they are still single when all their friends, cousins, nieces and nephews seem to be getting engaged, married or at least involved in committed relationships. They often ask, "Why them and not me? Why am I still single? What's wrong with me?" Since I have long believed that 80 percent of all questions are just statements in disguise, what they're really doing is saying, "There's nothing wrong with me. I shouldn't still be single. I'm good enough to be married."

But if you know anything about me, you know I don't always give people the answers they want. Whether it's a valid question or a statement in disguise, when somebody asks, "What's wrong with me?" rather than giving mindless support, I actually try to analyze and answer the question. You asked me what's wrong with you, so I'm going to check and see if there is something that others could perceive as wrong. Who knows? If you ask me, all I can do is lead you to the questions that will yield the answers you really need to create change. You cannot change what you do not acknowledge. Maybe you are unavailable or maybe you are boring. Maybe you behave like a complete doofus or nerd. (Notice I didn't say you *are* a nerd—and if you thought I did, that may make you oversensitive and a nerd—I said you might be behaving in a nerdy fashion.) Maybe you have really poor hygiene, have greasy hair and smell like a goat in a rainstorm, I don't know. But if you're asking the questions, you need to be prepared to really look for and deal with real and honest answers. If you have been single and searching for too darn long, maybe there is something wrong with how you *behave and present* yourself in the eyes of the people you are trying to attract. So let's take a good hard look at you.

Now you can read the preceding paragraph and think I'm some kind of a jerk for suggesting there really is something wrong with how you engage and interact with people. But I could be right. Maybe, maybe not. But if there is something, if you are shooting yourself in the foot every time you start dating, don't you want to figure out what you're doing and stop doing it? Otherwise, when it comes to romance, you'll keep limping along at best. I'm not trying to be rude or hurt your feelings. But I said that my goal is to get you results and I meant it. If what you want is to find the person that you want and deserve, then you may have to start doing things differently. You can't continue to use the same behaviors and skills that haven't worked so far and expect them to start working all of a sudden. You owe it to yourself to, at least, take a hard look. If you find nothing, then great—no problem.

So what are some of the behaviors that are keeping you single? If there is any part of you that thinks you have to have a man to be happy or you'll just curl up and die, I already know one thing that is keeping you single right there: You're desperate, and—trust me—that will scare men to death. Language can be a powerful thing. If you're telling yourself you're "desperate" and you "must" have a man, you will "reek" of fear, weakness and desperation. I've never heard of a guy who has those three qualities on his list of major turn-ons. It would be like a woman saying, "Well, the first thing I look for in a man is sexual ambiguity." And besides, if you're telling yourself you "must" have a man, then you are absolutely lying to yourself. I'm going to let you in on a little secret: There are very few "musts" in life. You must have air or you suffocate. If people can't get oxygen, they *are* desperate. They *must* fix that now. But this is no way to talk about a relationship. It's not do or die.

Now think of those people who are suffocating. They look panicked, right? All bug-eyed and tense. Well, guess what? That may be exactly how you look if you're telling yourself that you absolutely must find a husband.

Only 7 percent of all communication is verbal. The other 93 percent, the percent that is screaming what you are really feeling, is nonverbal. It's in your tone of voice, syntax, facial expression, muscle tension, body language and other physiology. And believe me, it isn't exactly subtle.

You may talk a good game, but I suspect that your body is fronting you out by the end of the first day. The desperation mind-set is self-defeating, and regardless of the shape he's in, any guy who sees or senses it will immediately beome a world-class sprinter and take off in the opposite direction.

You need to stop filling your mind with that kind of self-sabotaging drivel, because it is simply not true. You want to have a mate. It would be cool if you had a mate. It would be fun if you had a mate. You sure would appreciate it if you had a mate and you certainly hope that you will. But you don't *have* to have one. Once you've fixed your thinking, then you can begin breaking old desperate habits and presenting yourself as that defined product we discussed in Chapter 3.

Relationship Autopsy

If we are going to get real, then it's time to dissect your last relationship and your relationship patterns. The best predictor of future behavior is relevant past behavior—unless, of course, something major happens to change the flow of events. I want this book and this process to be that major happening. So let's take a really candid look over your shoulder and figure out what you've been doing to ensure a long and loveless life.

You can tell yourself it's bad luck, you can tell yourself you've been the victim, but if you want to make a change in your life, then you're going to have to tell yourself the truth: This is no time to blame your ex, bad timing or general incompatibilities. The buck stops here. With you.

Now don't get the wrong idea—I'm not saying that you are to blame or even that you are the only one with responsibility. But I'm focusing totally on you because you're the only one who's reading these words. You are the only one that I have any ability to influence. More important, you're the only one you really have any control over. So if you're going to get the relationship you want, it is going to be because of what you do. I am asking you to figure out what you did to get the results you didn't want, what you did to contribute to the problem, so you can begin to understand how you could have behaved better. You are going to learn from this experience. And you will get better at this relationship business, because you have the courage to be honest with yourself.

So let's start with your last relationship—whether that was a ten-year marriage or a ten-day fling. Ask yourself these questions.

1. *What were your problems and frustrations with the relationship?*
2. *What were the problems your partner had with you? Be honest with yourself.*
3. *What are ten key statements about the pain you still feel and the open wounds you still have? Write them down. Again, honesty is essential.*
4. *For each of the statements you just wrote down, ask yourself: What was my role in this?*
5. *What choices did you make that led to the results you got in your last relationship?*

6. *You teach people how to treat you. Did you teach your partner to treat you badly?*
7. *What do you have to change to get over your last relationship? How do you need to heal?*
8. *What part of your last relationship do you want to leave in the past forever? Only when you acknowledge it can you take the steps to prevent repetition.*
9. *You need emotional closure. To get that, you need to figure out what is your "minimal effective response"—the least thing you can do to get the closure. It may be yelling and screaming, writing your thoughts down or actually talking to your ex. If you need to take steps to feel that you've stood up for yourself, do it.*

Now that you've taken some time to look at your past relationships, you can figure out what part, if any, your own fear and anxiety played in the demise of those relationships. Maybe your fear of getting hurt caused you to panic and jump ship way too soon. Maybe you pushed him away with your unrealistic demands and expectations. In either case, your fear of being alone or your fear of getting hurt set off anxiety alarms, leading you to fight too hard or run too soon.

The most powerful motivator in all people is fear. It shouldn't be. We would hope the most powerful motivator would be something positive that would move you toward what you want, instead of away from what you don't want. It is an old adage in psychology that "what I fear I create." Some experts estimate that 80 percent of all choices are motivated by fear. It changes perception, it changes your behavior, it changes your reactivity, it changes you into a state of paranoid self-preservation that will contaminate any relationship you get into.

And the fear fuels your desperation. Not a good thing. You're like a hungry bird, screaming, "feed me, love me!" over and over again. There's no question about your willingness. But there is a constant demand, a pressure that makes men extremely uneasy. For the guy, it's like being audited by the IRS. All he wants to do is make sure he doesn't say the wrong thing—then get the heck out of there! If you've ever gone out with a desperate guy, you know the drill . . . the shrimp cocktail hasn't even arrived and he's already trying to pin you down for ten more dates. Desperate people are like leeches; they will suck you dry and then *still* not leave. They are bottomless pits for whom you can never do enough—and if you're desperate, you might as well say it in a personal ad, because it's that obvious.

If you are freaking out because your biological clock is ticking and you *must* get a mate now, trust me, you aren't much fun to date. You are probably about as subtle as a grizzly bear in heat—and about that attractive. You might as well suggest having your first date at Babies R Us.

Men read desperation only one way: *You don't have what you need, so you're going to take it from me.* "If she is lonely, she is going to take my independence and my free time. If she is unhappy, she is going to bring me down. I was happy before I met her. I am happy at a level ten. She is happy at level zero. Now I've suddenly gone from ten to five and I'm sinking fast. That's not what I'm looking for in a relationship. I'm better off by myself."

In relationships, men don't always start out with what you would call the most giving of attitudes. Men tend to start out much more selfishly, often looking for nurturing, comfort and service. Natural negotiators, men are always angling for the better end of the bargain. A prize. Not a job. So, if you are bored with your life and need somebody to entertain you, or if you're in full-blown baby panic mode, the man will home in on your sense of desperation and interpret that to mean you are trying to saddle him with a job. You've just assigned him the task of entertaining you or fathering your children. Trust me on this, most men don't go on a date with an eye toward getting assigned a second career. If you present yourself with desperate needs, I guarantee that the man you're having dinner with is going to be looking for the door, and the only happiness he'll find is seeing you in his rearview mirror. He's thinking, "I went out for some fun, but got a bunch of jobs at the most desperate level of urgency instead. That wasn't what I had in mind." Believe me when I tell you he will be gone in a heartbeat.

What you want him to be saying is, "What do I have to offer her?"—not "What is she going to take from me?" This is a big difference. I'm not accusing men of being forever selfish in relationships. I'm saying that they don't want to work for you; they want to date you. Don't worry, once he falls in love with you, he will take the job—and probably pad his résumé to boot. Once he decides that you are valuable and worth keeping around, he will look for ways to be meaningful to you. In fact, once a man falls in love, he starts looking for things that he can do to "earn" his keep. As I will discuss in Chapter 6, men are often intimidated if they feel they don't have something to offer a woman. Clearly, you have wants and needs. And those wants and needs can actually be positive elements when introduced in the right way at the right time. But that right time is never going to happen if you come on too desperate, too soon.

Are You Desperate?

Whether you know you're desperate or not, whether you are intending to come across that way or not, if you're telling yourself things like "I must," "I have to" and "It is a catastrophe if he doesn't love me," then you are putting yourself into a state of desperation and panic, a state that screams, "I need. I want." The state you need to be in to succeed is the state that can honestly reflect everything you want and value. It can also be a state that says, "I have a lot to give." The difference between these mental states is all about your internal reality and the kinds of things you've been telling yourself. Don't think that your social mask, your attempt to be "cool" about it, will fix the problem. You actually need to change what you are saying to yourself as well as how you think and feel. You need to relax, lighten up and realize that you don't "have to have" an ongoing relationship in order to be okay.

Look over the following list of statements

and circle all the ones that you've said to yourself or that apply to you:

1. *I must make this work because if I don't, I am a loser.*
2. *If I don't get married by thirty-five, I'll die alone.*
3. *I must be a loser because everybody in my family and life is getting into meaningful relationships but me.*
4. *There must be something wrong with me because no one asks me out a second time.*
5. *I need to please him in order to keep this relationship going, because it is so humiliating to be alone.*
6. *I need his approval or he will dump me like all the rest.*
7. *I really am an idiot in relationships.*
8. *If he loves and accepts me, then I can finally feel okay about myself.*
9. *I don't know when to stand up and assert myself, because I fear I might ruin the relationship.*
10. *I really want to tell my family and friends that I am successful in a relationship—especially that I am married to the right person.*

11. *I am afraid or depressed most of the time I am with someone, because I fear failure.*
12. *I never "live in the moment" and enjoy a relationship, because I am always worrying about whether or not there is a future with my partner.*
13. *I want to avoid pain at all costs, and I live in fear that my partner will hurt me.*
14. *No past relationships have worked out, so I never let myself believe that there is one that really will work.*
15. *I know he's going to leave me eventually, so I'll "get him" before he gets me.*
16. *I need reassurance, so I have to test him by pushing him away to see if he will prove that he cares by staying.*
17. *Relationships involve too much stress and drama.*
18. *I am not really good enough for him.*
19. *I hate myself most of the time in relationships.*
20. *I have to protect myself so that I will not get hurt again.*

If you've circled even three of the above statements, yes, you are desperate. You're either desperate to get a man, or desperate to avoid getting hurt.

The first step toward change is admitting that you have a problem.

If more of your circled statements are numbered 1 through 10, then you are desperately afraid of being alone. If more are numbered 11 through 20, then you fear getting hurt and losing your balance most of all. In either case, you're undermining your chances for the good relationship that I am assuming you want, given that you're sitting here reading this book.

The Many Faces of Desperation

The popular misconception is that all forms of desperation look alike. But fear elicits one of two responses—fight or flight. The fight reaction is what we usually associate with desperation. We think of women who become aggressive, maybe even predatory—the stalkers with fatal attractions, women who pursue relentlessly. But that's just one category.

There is an equally large percentage of women who react to anxiety by distancing themselves from any potential problems. Like the fighters, the flighters lack the patience to let a relationship progress naturally—except that instead of trying to escalate it, they actively seek to bring an end to the relationship and any feelings of discomfort they may be experiencing. One woman I know tests guys by not returning their phone calls. If they don't keep trying to reach her, she chalks it up to the fact that they're not interested and never sees them again. Meanwhile the guy whose calls have gone unanswered thinks he's been rejected and is baffled, since he doesn't know the reason.

See if you can recognize yourself in any of these faces of desperation:

- **You think you're past your prime—** If you believe in ageism, I can assure you that you are fueling it. Peers attract peers at every stage of the human life span. If you are good-looking at thirty-one and dating guys five years older, you'll be just as good-looking at fifty-one—to guys who are fifty-six! Now, if you're still longing for the thirty-six-year-old at that age—that is, someone fifteen years younger than you—and you don't look like Demi Moore, I agree, you may have a problem.
- **You're in a screaming emotional dive—**Your last relationship crashed and burned and you're looking for a new outlet for all your emotions while

the ashes of the old one are still smoldering. Choosing a mate when you are hurting ensures a shoddy selection process because you're moving away from pain, not toward a good partner. Once the hurt subsides and you've fully rebounded, you will look at the choice you made and realize he's just someone—as in, not the one for you.

- **You're watching your womb's biological clock**—After a certain age, many women develop the sense that their biological clocks have become hostile, volatile soup tyrants that could say "No baby for you!" at any moment. The resulting sense of urgency that you project scares men away and forces you into a compromised relationship that has little chance of succeeding. Having a baby with the wrong guy may be a good premise for a sitcom, but in real life it's going to mess up three people. Stop the stress and start taking the tips in this chapter to heart. (And, while you're at it, quit reading those alarmist articles your mother has been sending you!)

- **You're an independent woman—** You make your own money. You're used to being the boss. You don't play second fiddle to any guy. And you are scared to death of sharing your space with a partner after years of living alone. You think you're choosy, but you know that deep down, you're scared of messing up the good thing you've got going—with yourself. You may think you want a partner when what you really want is to leave well enough alone.
- **You're afraid to play with fire—** Maybe you've been burned too many times and you're feeling a little skittish around heat. Maybe several disappointments in rapid succession have got you thinking that a relationship is not in your cards, so why even bother? If you are afraid to get back up on that relationship horse, stick

with me, because I am going to show you how to tame that stallion and walk him safely to the barn.

- **You think you're fat and ugly—** Baloney! Who told you that? To the right guy, those extra pounds look like feminine curves. And while that face you see day in and day out may have worn out its welcome with you, in the eyes of the right man, it's unique, character-filled, quirky or wise.

Change Your Mind, Change Your Life

You have to be able to decide that you will be okay even if you never find the special someone you are looking for. This means deciding that if you have to be alone, you are not a bad person to do it with. It also means believing that in your most authentic state, you are absolutely worthy of having a committed partner of quality. And it means believing that by embracing the Character of You, you will most likely find that quality companion.

❤♡

Bottom line: Loving smart means believing in you, your worth and your value.

You need to know and believe that you can be and will be a winner.

Thinking like a winner, feeling like a winner and behaving like a winner are essential to victory. Do you think the world-class tennis player Venus Williams or the champion golfer Annika Sorenstam would ever have won so many top-level professional victories had either of them believed she was a loser and unworthy of the titles? Just as they are fine-tuned athletes, I want you to be a fine-tuned "date-lete," and to do that, you have to know when you're sabotaging yourself and how you can train yourself so you can go out there and hit them with your "I got it going on" attitude. You can show sincere interest, affection and an attitude marked by a willingness and desire to move forward in the relationship. What you can never show, if you ever hope to succeed, is a desperate need to go to the next level.

It will take commitment. Old habits die hard, but that's exactly what happens when you change your thoughts. When you realize you are in control of how you think, you learn that you are also in control of how you feel and how you behave and, by extension, how other people respond to you. That's what I often refer to as your locus of control, a sense of who is in charge of your life.

When it comes to dating, many women pass off their locus of control to the guy because of their negative self-talk and desperation. They externalize it. When you're in this state you feel that you're at the mercy of your dates—they can hurt you, make you happy, make you sad, make you crazy. If a guy gets your number and never calls, you may say: "It's because I talked about my job too much. My job is boring. I am boring. Why didn't I just let him talk? Stupid, stupid, stupid. I will never learn. Oh yeah, and I am too fat!"

If you've ever heard yourself say, "He makes me so mad," you're blaming someone else for your feelings and actions and externalizing your locus of control. Instead of taking responsibility for your thoughts, emotions and behavior, you say, "He's making me do this" as if you're nothing but a pawn in some guy's game. You have to ask yourself, Is *he* making you feel this way or are you making yourself feel this way? Nobody can make you feel anything. You are ultimately in command of how you feel. If he swore he'd call and didn't, you have one of three options. You can spend all day freaking out, calling him and leaving frantic messages in his voice mail—that's the fight response. Or you can take flight and decide that anyone so irresponsible isn't worth your while anyway. And finally, you can take a few deep breaths, chill out, realize that you don't have the faintest clue why he didn't call and shrug it off as one of life's little mysteries.

You see? Your feelings really are a product of your internal dialogue. If you're telling yourself that he didn't call because you're fat or boring, or because he has better things to do, all you're doing is hurting yourself. That becomes your reality.

You wouldn't say those things to a friend, so why are you talking to yourself as if your words have no consequences? They do. They get your adrenaline pumping, making you anxious and desperate for relief. The truth is you don't know why he didn't call, so why jump to negative conclusions—either about him or about yourself? From now on, whenever you're feeling anxious, panicked or down on yourself, sit down and identify the thoughts that run through your head. Write them down and put each through the following test:

1. *Would objective sources, maybe your friends or relatives who aren't so invested, think this thought is true?*
2. *Does this thought serve my best interests?*
3. *Is it healthy for me to maintain this thought?*
4. *Is this thought helping create an attitude that will get me what I want and deserve in a relationship?*

If you can't answer in the affirmative to all of the above questions—that's right, all of them—drop that thought right then and there. It's amazing how mean some women can be to themselves. And the consequences are disastrous. Just look at the difference between the actions of someone who is thinking realistically and someone whose thoughts are distorted by a destructive internal dialogue:

DESTRUCTIVE: *I don't look good without a tan.*
I feel insecure when I am pale.

REALISTIC: *I look great with a tan, but I'm still pretty without one.*
I am confident no matter what.

DESTRUCTIVE: *That guy just wants to talk to my friend.*
I'll let my friend do the talking.

REALISTIC: *I wonder if that guy is interested in me or my friend.*
I'll engage him in conversation and find out.

DESTRUCTIVE: *If he finds out that I'm not wealthy, he'll leave.*

I'll lie and put on an act to get him to stay.

REALISTIC: *If he needs to marry rich, we're not a match.*
I will be forthright about my financial status and see how he reacts.

DESTRUCTIVE: *He's just going to dump me like the others.*
I'm not going to get involved.

REALISTIC: *I don't know what is going to happen.*
I will give it time and see what develops.

Never Let Them See You Sweat

Here is where we replace the bad, male-repelling thoughts with the kind of stuff that will make you a man-magnet. A great self-image will beat out collagen injections and silicone implants every time. It's also a heck of a lot cheaper and more real; most guys don't want a long-term relationship with a woman who could have body parts recalled. If you want to show the world that you have everything to give and nothing to lose, follow the example of powerful people.

When tycoons like Donald Trump are negotiating a deal, they cannot act desperate. Believe me, the second they show their potential partner how bad they need the deal, the jig is up. They can wind up with the short end of the stick or blow the deal altogether.

To combat the sweaty-palms syndrome, successful entrepreneurs tell themselves something that every single girl should tell herself from date one: "Whatever happens, it's not going to change my life." What this means to you is that even though you don't connect with the current possibility, if you handle yourself well and you love smart, chances are you are going to have plenty of options and your life will go on just as it always did. What happens may even be a blessing in disguise.

To tell yourself this and really believe it, you have to take a step back and realize that the things you really enjoy, the things that give you the most pleasure and make life worth living, are all things you already have. A walk in the park with your dog. Some quality time with your friends. An hour in the sun—just you and your iPod. No man can give these things to you or take them away, so there's no reason to act as though the world will come to an end if that random conversation you struck up with Joe, the accountant at the Burger Doodle down on the corner, doesn't develop into a relationship.

When people are really confident, they are not hungry for external validation. They do not enter into a relationship looking for evidence as to whether they are okay or not. They have already held that debate—and won. They have done their personal audit and have made a decision on whether they are or are not mentally, spiritually and physically okay.

Confident people are calm without being aloof or arrogant. This sense of peace comes from an awareness of their authentic self, the part of you that can be found at your absolute core. It is the part of you that is not defined by your job, your function or your role. It is the composite of all your unique gifts, skills, abilities, interests, talents, insights and wisdom. It is all of your strengths and values that are uniquely yours and need expression, versus what you have been programmed to believe that you are supposed to be and do.

If you know who you are, if you are secure in who you are and, most important, if you accept who you are, then it will take a lot to knock you off your balance. If, on the other hand, you are unsure of yourself, you'll be very vulnerable to the whims of others. It could be something as minor as someone being rude to you in line at the grocery store. You may be offended all day, wondering, "Why would he treat me that way? Was it because he didn't think I was an important person?" But the truth is that if you already know who you are, you are neither validated nor deflated by what someone else does, because you haven't given your power to anyone else. You have kept your power and you know that you are the same person whether others are lavishing you with praise or ignoring you completely.

Remember, when it comes to looking confident, attitude is everything. Feeling secure and self-assured will guarantee that you come off that way. If you want to know what confidence looks and feels like, check out the following list. People who are obviously confident . . .

- ✔ May compare themselves with others, better-looking or not, but they'll always end up saying something like, "Well, yeah, she may have the great bod, but I've got the nice eyes and great sense of humor!" The way they look at themselves always makes them feel better about who they are in the end.
- ✔ Are as comfortable just standing back and listening as being the center of attention.
- ✔ Can keep their cool in every social situation, from the most flattering to the most awkward, because they know who they are and do not allow external events to dictate how they see themselves.
- ✔ Do what they have to do to feel good about their looks, whether that means working out, getting regular massages, or eating right.
- ✔ Do what they have to do to feel good about their brains. And that means

giving their all at work, always learning something new and reading, reading, reading.

- ✔ Understand that people respond to energy rather than looks. They focus on expanding their personality to get the attention.
- ✔ Make sure that they are taking their fair share of time in most conversations—50 percent in a twosome, 33 percent in a threesome, and so forth. If you're standing there nodding with a drink in your hand, you're becoming a bit player in a movie about you.
- ✔ Smile, laugh and look happy and engaged. That's what makes them approachable and the center of attention.
- ✔ Don't have a problem taking center stage. When the time comes for them to speak, they do so with a clear, definite voice, broad gestures and honest opinions.
- ✔ Are more concerned with what they think of the person they're speaking to than what that person thinks of them.

- ✔ Dress to turn heads. When it comes to stunning looks versus run-of-the-mill, middle-of-the-road looks, a confident person will always choose to look stunning.
- ✔ Make eye contact. Eye contact may be last on this list, but it's the number one most attractive thing about any man or woman.

Bring It On

I don't want to spend another minute talking about the old you, the you who used to check her messages every five seconds hoping some guy had called—or the you who sat home every Saturday thinking, "Woe is me. My life sucks. Nobody loves me." That girl is yesterday's news. She is over. Done. Moved and left no forwarding address.

The woman who's read this chapter and learned its lessons is the one who turns heads on the street, because she walks with pride and purpose. She knows she's got it going on and she pities the fool who doesn't get it. She is the new and improved you. And this is what you're thinking:

- I have a lot of love to give.
- Any guy would be lucky to talk to me.
- I am charming and entertaining.
- I am great company.
- I love being by myself.
- I am fabulous.
- I am a great catch.
- My life is complete.
- Is he good enough for me?
- What do I want?
- If I am not happy, I will leave.
- I am satisfied with who I've become.
- I have great friends, a wonderful family and people who love me.
- I have a great heart and a warm spirit.
- I have everything I need.
- I don't want anything from anyone.
- My happiness depends on me.
- Life is beautiful.
- Only I can change my life.
- There is so much more to me than my looks.
- I am wise and experienced.
- I am a beautiful human being.

If you can look at these statements and nod your head in agreement, it's official: You now have the kind of confidence that propels relationships forward. And I wouldn't be at all surprised if right at this moment you're looking back at your past dates and romances and shaking your head in wonder at how scared you once were—whether of getting hurt or being alone. If you can clearly see and feel great about the difference between how you approached relationships then and how you intend to approach them now, congratulations. You can start to do things differently.

5

Your Inner Bride

It is better to be looked over than overlooked.

MAE WEST

Now that you've got those nay saying saboteurs out of your system, it's time to figure out what is so wonderful about you. I mean, for all I know, you may actually be sitting there wondering, "Well, if I'm NOT a big ugly loser, then who and what in the world am I?" It's time for a personal inventory—using the character of you to create the defined product I talked about in Chapter 3. Now, if that means standing in front of the mirror and telling yourself that you've got flabby arms, crow's-feet and no fashion sense, then go back through Chapters 3 and 4 and read them again, because you are not ready for what we are about to do here. I am serious. I'm not going anywhere, and the words won't fall off these pages while you're gone. I'll be here if it takes a week. And this isn't just about how you look. Sure, looks matter, sometimes; but unless you are scaring the livestock—in which case, okay, maybe you need a new hairdo—you've got to do the best you can with what you have.

Okay, enough about that. Ready now? Good. Because, frankly, I don't know where I would be today had *my* twenty-two-year-old self said, "Your nose was broken seven times and is crooked," then checked out and lived behind the barn. Distinguishing yourself means accepting what you have and making the most of it. So if you have a little extra meat on your bones, be proud of your curves. Think sexy. And if you've got smile lines, consider them the charming proof of your happy, friendly disposition—and remember that you can smile naturally, because you haven't been Botoxed into looking like The Joker. You may never be the *Sports Illustrated* swimsuit model that every guy drools over, but 99.99 percent of the world's men don't marry *Sports Illustrated* swimsuit models, so no biggie.

To focus on your assets, you have to turn off your critical eye and turn on the lens that appreciates strong suits and good qualities. Then define yourself in terms of those traits. For example, if you are going to be the sexy demure woman, your wardrobe will be a whole lot different from what it would be if you planned to be the life of the party. The sexy demure girl comes to a Christmas party wearing a form-fitting dress and smoky eye makeup; the life of the party is the cutup who comes in an elf suit with fuzzy antlers tied to her head, antlers that have lights all over them. Is one better than the other? No. Just different like Neiman Marcus and Wal-Mart, like apples and oranges.

When you're trying to define yourself and carve out your niche in the social scene, it's all about what you have to offer. Once you start thinking in those terms, you'll see that there are four main areas that define any person's contribution to a relationship. I bet you've got more going on than you think.

1. *Presence and style*
2. *Personality*
3. *Content*
4. *Appearance*

These four areas combine to make you a very certain and specific type of person, partner and Character of You. Each of us makes a statement with the way we present ourselves, conduct ourselves and interact with others. If that statement is consciously selected and consistently advanced, it has tremendous power.

Conscious selection is what we are doing right now. And what I need you to discover during the course of this personal inventory is who you really are: a great partner, a fantastic catch and one of the world's best-kept secrets.

As we discuss the different aspects that go into your persona, I will periodically remind you to consider your own best attributes, and recognize the ones you may have been ignoring and taking for granted all along. Once you are fully aware of and duly awed by your own fine qualities, they will provide a foundation of confidence for the bridge that will connect you to other people.

---

1. Presence: Can You Connect?

While your appearance is what makes people curious to get to know you, your presence is what makes them respond to you. This is what's often referred to as your energy, your spirit, your vibe and your aura. Think of it this way: Your appearance is what makes you look good on paper; your presence is what helps you jump off the page. This area includes all those qualities that help you bond with another human being. It starts with eye contact and moves into your listening skills as well as the extent to which you're engaged in dialogue or social interaction. Some people are always there, giving you 100 percent; others will give 20 percent at best because their minds are in a million places at once. Which type are you?

Your touch also falls into the category of presence. The way you make physical contact with a man speaks volumes, communicating everything from rejection and fear to intimacy and nurturing. Your movements and the way you carry yourself when sitting, standing or dancing all contribute to your overall presence.

A new Dartmouth University study just confirmed what I've been saying all along: Women who can hold a man's gaze are seen not only as much more attractive but as much more likable.

Eye contact, is an especially powerful presentation tool. Very few people have the ability to make eye contact. So long as you're making eye contact while you're talking, people are entranced. It doesn't even matter what you're saying. If you're already good at eye contact, you don't need me or a study to tell you that women who can walk up to a guy and lock eyes can create a very intense, personal bond in a very short time.

When it comes to relationships, your presence is no small offering. Of all the things you have to give, this is the one that will ensure that your partner doesn't feel alone in the world. And when you stop to think about it, isn't that ultimately the one thing that anybody really wants out of a mate?

Now, as you choose what type of presence you want to radiate in a room, you have to consider who you are as a person. If what you did in the past just straight up didn't work, then it's time to commit to making a change. You must learn to adapt. Don't just show up at a social situation. Show up with a plan—and we will create one in Chapter 7. It can be as detailed and hammered-out as determining when you arrive (early to get the home-court advantage, or fashionably late to build anticipation), where you stand or sit (are you on the couch or in the kitchen mixing drinks?), how you interact with people (do you approach first, wait to be recognized, mingle with many, focus on a few?) and what kind of humility or confidence you radiate (are you going to talk about yourself or ask others questions? Stand up straight in the center of the room, or slouch against a wall? Laugh really loud and smile a lot, or brood and simmer the night away?). So, yes, if hanging out at the buffet chatting up the deli meats hasn't been working for you, then you have got to step away from the cold cuts and force yourself to be yourself despite any initial feelings of anxiety that you may experience.

The following traits define your presence. Which ones can you flaunt?

Intuition
Empathy
Listening
Attentiveness
Compassion
Sensitivity
Tact
Understanding
Poise
Cheerfulness
Nonjudgmental attitude
Inquisitiveness
Curiosity
Interest
Communicative
Consideration
Knowing when not to speak
Eye contact

Trust
Passion
Focus
Ability to tune in
Adaptability
Social sensitivity
Style of engagement
Sense of authority
Warmth
Rhythm
High energy

2. Personality: What You Bring to the Table

We all have a way of being in the world, and we generally call that way our personality. There is a broad range of characteristics that lie on this continuum, and many will simply not feel authentic. For example, the role of cheerleader is simply outside my range. I am well aware that in some instances, a cheerleader is what's called for. So in those cases, I just stay away.

You have already defined the Character of Him. Now you need to find the characteristics that make up your own personality. Given what you've learned about who you want, now you can begin to develop your personality to complement the kind of partner you would like to wind up with. For instance, if you decide you want someone who lives on the edge and is a bit unpredictable, you may need to scale back your desire to schedule every last minute of your day. This is not a quality that will serve you well in a relationship with a guy who is all about living in the moment. I am not saying you let him control the course of the entire relationship. I am saying that you have decided what you want in a guy—I didn't decide it for you, the guys you meet won't be deciding it for you, it's all you—and either you're going to do what it takes to get it or you're not.

The realm of personality also includes your style of companionship—all those characteristics that will make you compatible with one person and incompatible with another. These are the actions that show him and yourself what kind of team you can be and the future possibilities you can achieve together. Everything from your skills and strengths to your basic and most salient characteristics falls under this category. Companionship is what makes a relationship's course run smoothly simply because you two have complementary strengths.

The point is that when it comes to presenting yourself as a life partner, you had better know what your strengths are because you may very well have to use them to fill in for your partner's shortcomings. Your nurturing style is also a very important part of your personality spectrum. If you can't think of anything you'd rather do than plan your investment portfolio and watch the stock market, while your partner thinks "price-earnings ratio" is Latin for "wake me when it's over," you can nurture your partner by taking care of the financial planning.

When you're trying to figure out what your nurturing skills are, consider how you behave toward your family, friends and even coworkers when they are depressed, sick or just having an off day. Also, think about what you do for people without expecting anything in return. Maybe you're the type of person who chooses to leave the last piece of calamari for your friend, even if you really want it yourself. Or it could be that you're a great cook with a killer BBQ recipe. Maybe you're very supportive and will just as soon compliment your colleague on her hair, clothes and jewelry as say, "Hey, how's your job going?" In fact, you could be taking care of people all the time by giving them your respect, consideration and positive regard.

It's the way we make people feel that ultimately determines the longevity and quality of our relationships. Figuring out what you have to offer in terms of companionship and nurturing skills can be challenging. Look over this list and let it inspire you to come up with new insights into your personality:

Funny	*Assertive*
Intelligent	*Passive*
Well-mannered	*Optimistic*
Honest	*Practical*
Loyal	*Positive*
Aggressive	*Planner*
Numbers Cruncher	*Great Cook*
Affectionate	*Pillar of Strength*
Appreciative	*Selfless*
Patient	*Supportive*
Energetic	*Committed*
Defender	

3. Content

The character of you is going to be significantly reflected and exhibited by the content of what you talk about and are interested in. For example, you'll make a very different statement if you meet somebody and your first question is, "Where do you work out?" versus, "Do you think Senate confirmation hearings get too contentious?"

I'm not saying that one question is better than the other, or that either is a great example of the kind of content you want to convey, but I do want to point out the different messages the two approaches send. This category is where you decide what type of knowledge and information interests you and matters to you. Here is where you embrace your values and beliefs and begin reflecting them in the conversations you have, the activities you choose and the interests you pursue.

Just remember, as with every other aspect of the character of you, your content should be congruent with who you authentically are. You cannot write the Character of You in such a way that you are being pseudo-intellectual—particularly if you thought "pseudo" began with an "s." That would be trying to be something you're not, and I just spent an entire chapter talking about what all is wrong with that approach. If you'd like another example, just think of that guy who barely made it through high school and has a very limited vocabulary, but persists in using and massacring big and sophisticated words in an effort to impress. What is more awkward than that—except knowing he's probably somebody's boss?

Your content should reflect who you truly are and what your interests truly are, not what you think others would be interested in. If a particular guy is turned off by that or doesn't like it, you are better off knowing that now, before you have two kids and one divorce attorney. So go through the following list and circle the interests that represent you, then feel free to dwell on the subject and add even more.

Pop culture	*Family*
Art	*Animals*
Music	*Travel*
Playing sports	*Cars*
Exercise	*Conspiracy theories*
Astrology	*Your work*
Social issues	*Fashion*
Politics	*Celebrity gossip*
History	*Current events*
Science	*Literature*
Business	*Spectator sports*
Shopping	*People and relationships*

One of the biggest misconceptions among singles is that appearance is all about physical looks. That is only a small fraction of what I mean by appearance. Don't get me wrong—men are visual beings. They fall in love with their eyes. Blame it on the thousands of years they spent as hunters and gatherers, making their eyesight into the sharpest sense. They are not interested in words so much as they are in actions that they can see. And they are not going to waste their time pursuing a woman when all appearances signal "proceed with caution."

Your physical appearance—including fashion, grooming, body shape and size, hair and makeup and even such accessories as shoes, jewelry and eyewear—can hugely contribute to the persona that reflects the Character of You. To succeed, you have to develop some social sensitivity and look around you to see how other people present themselves in an appropriate and appealing way. And I'm not talking about trying to be somebody you're not. I am talking about putting your best presentation forward. Again, you have to be willing to change what you're doing, within the range of who you authentically are, if what you're doing is not working. If your hair looks as though you just walked off the set of *Dynasty* and you think elastic waistbands are the answer to all of life's little wardrobe problems, you need to acknowledge that your appearance not only is out of style but may in fact be sending a very negative signal.

Just to be clear, this is not about saying that one look is better than another. It's about what works versus what doesn't. If what you're doing isn't turning any heads, you need to change it. Don't keep beating your head against the wall with the same threadworn routine. You need to be willing to change and adapt to the situation.

Contrary to popular belief, appearance goes well beyond your hair, clothes and bra size. By outward appearance, I am also referring to the whole experience a man has when he meets you. It's your auditory appearance, meaning how you speak, your accent, your vocabulary, the tone of your voice. It's your olfactory appearance, as in your scent, everything from your natural smell to the perfume you wear to the lotion you use.

I want you to go through the list of qualities that fall under appearance and identify specific things that are your strong points. If there is something we haven't covered—say, you think you have an especially fetching pinkie toe—go ahead and write it in yourself. Don't be afraid to emphasize any of your outstanding physical qualities, because these are what will get you noticed.

Your appearance is the most obvious set of characteristics that set you apart from

Legs	*Curves*
Hairstyle	*Fitness*
Jewelry	*Height*
Derriere	*Teeth*
Breasts	*Fashion*
Smile	*Eyewear*
Eyes	*Voice*
Hands	*Vocabulary*
Face	*Figure or physique*
Nose	*Back*
Hair color	*Neck*
Style	*Smell*
Skin	___ . . .

the rest of the world. And, fortunately, there is no shortage of changes you can make to improve that aspect. You can help yourself by looking at fashion magazines, by talking to trusted friends and by just being socially aware as to what seems to be the order of the day. Look around and see what the well-dressed people are wearing, how they're doing their hair, what kind of makeup they've got on. We've all seen people of both sexes who dress like the cast of *Friends*, but have the physiques of the cast of *Roseanne*. It just doesn't work, and if what you're doing isn't working, find the statement that is consistent and congruent with your personal truth and the character of you, and embrace a new look.

So go ahead and give yourself a good, long once-over. What do you see? There is research that says what men respond to is not actual size or measurement but the ratio of waist to hips. The hourglass can be large but if proportional, it is still appealing to most men. For example, Marilyn Monroe was voluptuous, so was Jane Russell. Or do you have great taste and a warm, gregarious personality? Have a party at your beautifully decorated home and play the hostess for all its worth. The point is to capitalize on and exploit your resources as much as possible. Begin to associate your outward appearance with your positive characteristics—whether your waist, your sense of humor, your hospitality, or all of the above. You will need to keep these highlights at the forefront of your mind because they are your most salient assets. They are what will get you noticed and in the door.

The Seven Qualities of Health-Engendering Women

Some people have the uncanny ability to spread good vibes wherever they go. They know how to bring the best out of you with the deft touch of David Copperfield. When you're with them, you always feel good about yourself, them and the world around you. If you can become this type of health-engendering woman, you will never again have a problem attracting men.

1. They see the strengths, not the limitations, in others and call the strengths forward. These are the people who will make you proud to be yourself because they will tell you why you are special.
2. They trust you to the point that you have to answer their expectations. Consequently they make you better than you normally are, and you can be proud of yourself.
3. They respect you for what you have done and where you have come from. They can see that you have experienced something real and respect you for your courage.
4. They are authentic in themselves and do not call for you to lie to them out of pride. They live by their rules and do not expect you to follow theirs.
5. They are at peace with themselves because they are not proving anything to you.
6. They are good listeners and sincere

in their interest in you. You feel important.

7. *They are available for honest and genuine discussion, making you want to share yourself.*

Action Steps

Before embarking on a relationship, men want to feel they are getting into something good. No guy wants to get involved with a girl who'll tell him about her mother's financial problems, her dependence on Prozac and her psychotic ex on the first date. And it's not that men don't like women with problems. People have problems. That's fine. It's just that no one wants to hitch his wagon to a person who can't go one night without being negative.

In this final section, I show you how to walk the talk. Take the following steps to implement the lessons learned in this chapter and—using everything you learned about yourself in the last few pages—become the kind of woman who gets noticed for the right reasons.

✔ 1. Determine your personal truth, as I discussed in Chapter 3: Keep calling yourself out on any self-hating or destructive messages you may have running through your mind. Talk it through with a friend, relative, preacher or professional if you have to; just make sure that clarion voice in your head is screaming, "You've got it" and not "You don't."

✔ 2. Create your sound bite: Explain who you are in twenty words or less. Make yourself sound as exciting as possible. Hit all your strongest attributes and exclude anything that sounds negative. For instance:

"I am a fit, attractive entrepreneur who always manages to make time for my family and friends."

Consider this sound bite your identity and let that be the face you show the world. If you've ever cringed at the prospect of a roundtable introduction—you know, the one where you have to give your name and say a little something about yourself before moving on to the next person—this is the step for you. Once you have your sound bite ready, you'll be able to face any room—whether it's a boardroom or a ballroom.

✔ 3. Write an online dating profile. (I give you some tips from the experts on doing this in Chapter 8). Even if you are not interested in Internet dating, consider this step practice in self-promotion. After all, online dating is all about marketing yourself. That's why they call the ads personals. If you're having a hard time coming up with things to say, then you are still not clear about your product. Go back over your personal inventory, then write an essay that illustrates your findings. That, in a nutshell, is your online dater's profile.

✔ 4. Dispel negative myths. Take the negative quality that bothers you the most and turn it into a positive. It could be that you don't think you're living up to your career potential. Or maybe you don't have as many friends as you'd like. Whatever this so-called flaw, stop and consider what choices you made to get you to this point—and why. Maybe you expect a lot of your friends and are independent enough not to stay in an unrewarding relationship. Maybe your career gives you a great deal of personal freedom and lets you lead a stress-free life. See? Suddenly, even being unmotivated and unpopular doesn't seem so bad.

✔ 5. Banish your mental bully: Let's face it, nobody is perfect. But if we all walked around brooding over our shortcomings instead of thinking about our long suits, we'd be a world of mopers; we'd all be seventeen-year-old boys dressed in black T-shirts and jeans, our heads down, saying, "It's not fair." Focus on the many assets you discovered during this chapter whenever you want to boost your confidence and make a good impression.

✔ 6. Test your confidence: When you walk down the street and people look your way, ask yourself, "What are they looking at?" If you assume that the reason is anything other than positive and jump to the conclusion that people are staring at you because your pants are out of style, your thighs are fat, or your hair is a mess, go back to your personal inventory and come up with a new answer.

A Brand-New Defined Product

Bottom line: Good, bad or indifferent, you are who you are. The more aware you are of that person, the better able you will be to put that out there. You can look like a movie star and have everything going for you in the appearance department, but if you still haven't figured out the impression you're making on men and how to work it to your advantage, you're going to fade away fast. Trust me, you'll be sitting around wondering why a knockout like you can't get a guy when Plain Jane is hanging on the arm of Mr. *GQ* cover.

Use this chapter to recognize your own unique character, hone it to smooth-running perfection and then work everything you've got every chance you get. It's all about being remembered. They can love you or they can hate you, but one thing they will never do is forget you. There is someone who will find your character attractive. You may be the cerebral lawyer type like Miranda in *Sex and the City*, or you may be the man-eater like Samantha. That's your defined product and it's what will make people stop what they're doing to wonder about who you are and where you came from when you walk into a room.

Instead of sitting around, ignoring yourself and hoping good things will happen, I want you to start *making* things happen. You can begin with this speech:

"I'm tired of being a fly on the wall. I'm tired of fading into the background. I'm tired of being invisible. I'm tired of being left behind. That's not going to happen again. I'm going to do something else. Good, bad or indifferent, I am who I am. I'm going to take the best of what I've got and make people take notice. If it is my smile and my sense of humor, then all right. I'm going to quit whining about what I don't have and start flashing that smile and laughing with the happiest people in the room. People are going to remember me tomorrow! If the difference between winners and losers is that winners do things that losers won't do, then I'm going to be a winner. I'll take chances others won't take and I'll create what I want in my life. And I'm going to do it right now!"

6

Your Guy-Q

Men don't like to cuddle. We only like it if it leads to . . . you know . . . lower cuddling.

RAY BARONE, *EVERYBODY LOVES RAYMOND*

About a month before our youngest son, Jordan, left for college at SMU, thus rendering us "empty nesters," Robin started exhibiting some warning signs that let me know this was not going to be the easiest few months of our married life. She was nervous, often one blink away from tears and not the least bit interested in discussing the situation. One night, I awoke at around 3 A.M. to the sounds and vibrations of her quietly crying in bed next to me. Now I may not be the sharpest pencil in the box, but I have studied relationships in general and women in particular for years and I figure I'm no dummy, right? I also figure that along the way I've learned a few things about how women work, what they want and need and when they want and need it. One of the things I have "learned" is that women are often frustrated by men who always feel they have to jump in and fix everything. Lending a supportive spirit, being a shoulder to cry on and just being there would do a whole lot better.

Given that knowledge, I decided that the best thing for me to do would be to just slip an arm around her and quietly hold her. It seemed to be working, because she calmed down. Everything seemed to be fine and I thought, "Phew, dodged a bullet on that one and didn't have to say a word. Knowledge is power!" A few minutes went by and just as I drifted back off to sleep all smug and proud of my "night moves," she sat straight up in bed, flipped on the light, looked at me and said, "That's it? That's it? I am married to Dr. Phil, and I'm upset and crying in the middle of the night, and that's all you got?

What a crock!" So much for my understanding of the opposite sex!

How about you? How much do you understand about the other half?

If you've gotten this far and are still considering "acquiring" an adult human male, pay attention, because here is where I get down to brass tacks and tell you what you really want to know: what men really want, and how men think. I want to be like the behind-the-scenes stage manager who will tell you how they really cut the woman in half or turn the bouquet of flowers into a chicken—one of the many mysteries of life that have always perplexed me!

I'm betting that men are as much a mystery to women as women are to men. I mean, if you seriously think the way to a man's heart is through his stomach, some macho guys might tell you that may be aiming way too high. Interestingly enough, you may actually be aiming way too low, because you also have to understand how men think. Making him breakfast in the morning isn't going to get you a reservation for dinner later that night, or that week even, so stop bending over backward and slaving over a hot stove just to give him what he can get at the deli for $1.99.

I've got some news for you: Men and women are different. The upshot is that men are not all that complicated! You could read them like a book if you had a few very basic instructions and understandings. You need to know what drives them, what makes them do what they do when they do it and not do what they don't do when they don't do it. You don't have to read their minds, although you probably already think you do—and I have to admit that I sometimes think Robin is some kind of "Betazoid" when she seems to know what I'm thinking before I even realize I'm thinking it. (I hate it when she does that!) But with her help (and my surrender) I am, in this chapter, going to teach you just how that's done and what you absolutely, positively need to understand about the inner workings of a man to get that boy to do what you want him to do when you want him to do it—including making a commitment beyond saying, "Okay, see you Saturday if the good Lord's willing, the creek don't rise, and I don't get offered a ticket to the game."

When most of you try to figure out what in the world Billy boy was thinking when he looked deep into your eyes and said he could spend the rest of his life with you, then spent the next two weeks not calling, you get aggravated. How could he? The nerve! I would never do that. What kind of a person would do that to someone? *What a horrible, lying piece of crap!* And that is your first and most crucial mistake: You are using your own behavior and thinking as a yardstick.

The first step that you need to take in mastering the male mentality, the male hydraulics of cause-and-effect, is to understand and embrace the fact that female logic will not unlock the mysteries of male motivation.

You cannot use your experience base, your feminine reasoning or your powers of deduction to understand how men are wired up and why they do the things they do. By the way, it doesn't work in the other direction, either. Like my dad semijokingly said, there are two times when a man doesn't understand a woman: before marriage and after marriage. Men cannot apply their linear logic to understanding the emotional intricacies and intuition of the female. They invariably evaluate and judge female behavior trying to use a male yardstick. That doesn't even almost work.

If you need any proof of the difference, just check out some conversations. I heard a comedian capture it well—check out the way women interact with other women.

KAREN: *I love your new haircut! It's the cutest thing I've ever seen!*

DIANE: *Do you really think so? I wasn't sure when I first saw it. You don't think it's too short?*

KAREN: *Oh, no! It's absolutely perfect for you! I would love to get my hair to look like that, but my face is too fat so I'm stuck with this bird's nest.*

DIANE: *Are you serious? You are a stick figure and your hair is amazing!*

KAREN: *Are you kidding me? If I'm a stick then you must be invisible! And I'd give my right eye to be half as pretty! But thanks, I'm so glad you like this haircut!*

Now here's how two guys would play out that same conversation:

JOHN: *Haircut?*

JEFF: *Yep.*

That's a key difference between men and women. Women use an average of 7,000 words per day; men 2,000 words per day. Men also differ in their emotionality and reactivity. If someone forgets to invite a guy to a party, he or she can still be his friend. The same isn't necessarily true for women. It's not that he doesn't like your company or your haircut; it's just that he doesn't put a lot of energy into the details. Women don't understand that men forget things all the time. It's not meant to hurt your feelings. If you use the female sensitivity scale to measure men and take everything that seems like a violation personally you are going to be so frustrated that you will never make a connection.

I grew up with three sisters, and I know that girls can be just as sarcastic as guys. Some of the favorite barbs that I've seen, heard and read I have to admit are actually pretty funny even if they are a little "too close for comfort":

- He would be out of his depth in a birdbath.
- If he were any dumber, he would have to be watered twice a week.
- If he moved out of Idiotville the average IQ would go up.
- There is no way that guy should be allowed to breed.
- You don't need to know what he looks like to pick him out of a group. If there are four people there, and three of them look bored, he's the other one.
- I pinned a note to his shirt and sent him on his way.
- He has delusions of adequacy.
- I feel so sorry for his parents.
- We went to dinner and all I could

> think about was keeping my hands and feet away from his mouth.

Like I said, "a little too close to home." Now since I've been around the types of guys that I think these comments are meant to describe, I have to admit, they aren't all deep thinkers. Then again, are they all that bad or are they just being graded on the wrong scale? Real problems arise when either men or women allow their own, deeply entrenched and heavily socialized point of view create expectations about their partners. Case in point: Robin and I made the mistake of playing mixed doubles together one time. Get what I just said? We did it ONE TIME. We aren't over it yet! Robin took up tennis when I met her. But we played for different reasons. I play because I love competition. She played because she thought the clothes were cute. Now don't write in calling me a chauvinist. She said, and I quote, "I'm going to play because I would really look cute in that." So, I thought, okay, I'll get us into a mixed doubles league together.

We're playing this couple, and they've

got these lizard-belly tans like they've never seen the sun. And it's August in Texas! I mean, it's so hot, you can look out in your yard and see your dog burst into flames. So I'm thinking, these guys are way out of shape, it is stupid hot, we'll dehydrate them in no time. It gets better when I hear them say, "Oh, we forgot our water." Yes! Then I hear Robin say, "Well, here, drink some of ours." I can't believe my ears. I'm thinking, "WHAT? Why don't you just kiss 'em?"

Then we're in the middle of a point and the ball comes right to her. I mean, it was five inches from her foot. She doesn't even flinch, let alone try to hit it. I look at her to see what's the matter. She says, "What are you glaring at?" "I didn't say anything." Next ball, same thing—goes right by her. I say, "Why didn't you hit it?" And she says, "You get it, big shot. I was too busy being glared at." I could have choked her, and I am fairly certain she did try to kill me on at least two occasions since then. Just kidding! But I guess that's why they say coaching your wife is like trying to baptize a cat. Nobody wins. We aren't over it yet, and that was fifteen years ago! Live and learn.

Some women are very competitive and some aren't. Robin definitely falls in the "aren't" column when it comes to sports. Over the years she has been frustrated with me for not being "sensitive" or emotional in certain situations, and I have been frustrated with her for being too sensitive and emotional in certain situations.

I could have saved myself years of frustration if I had only understood that Robin was only doing what God had designed her to do. And she could have saved herself a lot of turmoil if she'd understood sooner that I was being true to my own nature, and she could not necessarily use her feminine yardstick to evaluate my male behavior.

So what does a woman need to understand the inner workings of the male mind? In this chapter, I break the male code of silence and fill you in on what's been going on behind closed doors. (Each of you readers can insert your own smart remark about how narrow those doors should be.) Warning: After I'm through telling you what's what, you're not necessarily going to like these poor schlubs any more, but you just may understand where they're coming from and stop taking everything they do personally. That's right—the good news is that it's not all about you or a lack of appreciation for you. The bad news is that men are men, and that this is not likely to change by any huge amount. They are trainable, but they are still men with male needs. Here's where you learn what these needs are.

Just a note of caution: Obviously I am generalizing. There is a broad range of differences among and between men. The male species is made up of individuals, and that means an infinite number of individual differences. Men are not all the same. Some are more emotional than others, some are more sensitive than others and some are just more in touch with their feminine side than others. What I'm about to tell you is true more often than not because there are some common trends—and some commonly held positions, values and beliefs. All of us can come up with exceptions to everything I am about to say. But if you embrace this knowledge as *generally* true, you will do pretty well in understanding what makes guys guys.

Fact or Fiction

Before I start telling you about how a lot of men operate, I want to know how much you already know about men. Strike that—I want *you* to know how much you actually know about men versus how much you only think you know. As I have said, most women labor under an unbelievable amount of delusions as to why guys do what they do. If you're going to get anywhere with a man, you need to separate the fact from the fiction. Then, I'll tell you how to increase your Guy-Q so that once you do find a great guy and bring him home, you can keep him there without either one of you driving the other one nuts.

So here's a quick quiz. See if you can separate the facts from the fiction:

1. *All men ever think about is sex—Fact or Fiction?*
2. *Men habitually run from or avoid commitment and are all wannabe players—Fact or Fiction?*
3. *Men grow up to be just like their fathers—Fact or Fiction?*

4. *Men compare every woman to their mother—Fact or Fiction?*
5. *Men are insensitive, inconsiderate jerks—Fact or Fiction?*
6. *Men need to feel like the leader in relationships—Fact or Fiction?*
7. *Men think it's weak to acknowledge needs—Fact or Fiction?*
8. *Men want only what they can't have—Fact or Fiction?*
9. *Men are intimidated by strong women—Fact or Fiction?*
10. *Men are selfish—Fact or Fiction?*

---

1. All men ever think about is sex.

I know, I know . . . you're probably thinking, "Okay, Doc, what is this—some kind of trick question? This is low-hanging fruit! Of course sex is all men ever think about." Well, it's not that simple. For men, sex is a very high priority. You may as well know this now.

When responding to anonymous surveys, men confess that one of the first things that goes through their mind when they meet a woman is what kind of sexual partner she would make. But women confess to jumping to conclusions as well—instead of sex they report that they consider what kind of a husband, partner or provider a guy might make. In the first split second, men take in chest, waist, hips—in other words, curves—whereas women see hair, clothes, posture, grooming and other external markers of stability and success.

But as you well know, even though sex is at the top of the man's list and security might be at or near the top for many women, neither of these priorities is anywhere close to all-inclusive.

Bottom line: FICTION. Sex is NOT all men ever think about. It definitely makes the short list, but it is not their singular focus, and in fact does not remain at the top of the list for very long. Which leads us to the next statement . . .

---

2. Men habitually run from or avoid commitment and are all wannabe players.

I've heard countless women complain about guys who aren't up for a relationship, but believe me, a time comes in most men's lives when the idea of chasing women, or even being chased by women, loses its sex appeal, ceases to feed their egos and fails to motivate them as a core priority in life. Of course that doesn't apply to all guys. There are some sexagenarians out there still sowing their wild oats. Many more men, however, are genuinely searching for a partner with substantive presence and companionship skills.

Like women, men also crave acceptance, validation, companionship and family and want to feel sexy, desirable and interesting. Just like women, men fall in love, and when they do they typically fall very hard. It is all about timing, both short- and long-term. If a man is burned out on the dating circuit and tired of starting over and over again, he is a prime candidate to settle down and make a commitment. If he is still playing the field and is measuring his virility by the number of women he can "conquer," then you couldn't snag him if you were the sole heir to the La-Z-Boy recliner factory. However, if he is ready and you're the one, you couldn't outrun him if you tried.

Bottom line: FICTION. Men do NOT want to be lifelong players and commitmentphobes, but as we will discuss later in the chapter, it is all about timing.

---

3. Men grow up to be just like their fathers.

The apple does not fall far from the tree. The acorn becomes the oak. However you slice it, if you want to understand a guy, take a close look at his father. If his father was loving and nurturing, bingo—chances are he will be as well. If the father was the "don't let that beer get warm on the way to my lazy behind" type, the sons will more likely than not copy at least some of those behaviors because that is what they learned and saw demonstrated from day one. All people tend to be affected by what they see and live rather than by what they don't see and live. Of course, there are exceptions; sons can consciously choose a path or course in life different from their fathers. Sometimes it is rebellion that motivates the change, sometimes it is pain from having to live with that which is considered to be negative and sometimes it is just a hunger for individuation.

Bottom line: FACT. Men do frequently

grow up with values and beliefs that reflect the father figure in their life. But exceptions can and do occur.

---

4. Men compare every woman to their mother.

By time you meet a guy, he's already had at least a twenty-year relationship with his mother. No matter how long his other relationships have been, the one he has with his mother is the most powerful and prominent. It's his anchor relationship, and to ignore that is foolhardy. If he's had a healthy relationship and he was taught to treat women with respect, that bodes well for you. If he was a complete taker and was never held accountable for anything, not so much.

Don't be oblivious of these dynamics or you will have a heck of a time trying to redefine your relationship. If your guy is expecting you to take over for the mom who never stopped treating him like a five-year-old, then roll up your sleeves because he's going to be leaving his dirty socks lying around, staying out late without checking in and whining up a storm when dinner isn't on the table in time for his first hunger pang. If he resents his mother for abusing or leaving his father, you may be paying for the sins of a woman who came before you. If he watched his mother in a warm, supportive and accepting relationship with his father, you may reap the benefits of a woman that came before you. But make no mistake, she was a powerful influence and she can and will have an impact on how he relates to you. Is a bad maternal history a deal breaker? Not necessarily, but you may have to negotiate a new deal and mutually define a relationship that is more amenable to your needs. Believe me, in the romantic relationship you have incentive power to influence him that momma just didn't have.

Bottom line: FACT. Men do tend to use their relationship with their mother as a compass in determining their relationship with the women in their lives.

---

5. Men are insensitive, inconsiderate jerks.

Okay, maybe you can come up with a lot of examples to support this contention, but is the belief generally true or has it been advanced by women who have had the misfortune of meeting some of those individuals who, shall we say, have come from the shallow end of the male gene pool? Or maybe the belief has been, at least in part, espoused by women who are making the mistake of measuring a man with a female rather than male yardstick. The truth is there are men who are insensitive jerks, just as there are women who are. It's also true that men have lower levels of sensitivity and responsiveness to situations that women might find more emotional. But this does not mean that men are all heartless. Men are "wired" differently hormonally and neurologically, and have been socialized differently from birth. Men have been designed and socially trained to be less sensitive and emotional because they were expected to do jobs that necessitated less emotional reactivity. Now, that doesn't make them better or worse than women; it just makes them different. The point here is that it isn't right or wrong. It's just the way it is.

So maybe the truth is that men *are* insensitive, but only if you're comparing them to the way you all carry on with your girlfriends, mothers and sisters. When guys are in the locker room, they're calling each other "butthead" and "scumbag"—and those are terms of endearment! Meanwhile, women are hugging each other, listening intently and comfortably supporting each other with sensitivity.

Bottom line: FICTION. Men don't care any less; they just respond less and express less. Different isn't bad—it is just different.

How a Man Differs from a Woman

You have to admit sometimes that differences in how we see each other are pretty funny:

- His phone conversations last about fifteen seconds.
- When watching TV he doesn't have to stop on every show that has someone crying.
- Chocolate is just another snack.

- Three pairs of shoes are more than enough.
- He can watch a game with his buddy for hours, not say ten words and part without hurt feelings.
- He can drop by to see a friend without calling ahead or bringing a little gift with a bow.
- If he doesn't call his buddy for a few days his buddy won't tell all their friends that he's changed.
- He never hears a buddy say, "So, notice anything different?"

Adapted from the *Greatest Joke Book Ever* by Mel Greene

---

6. Men need to feel like the leader in relationships.

Some men have been socialized to believe that they should take charge. They have been taught to believe that this is what is expected and required. On the basis of ego and machismo some (maybe most men) need to feel that they are in the driver's seat where their personal lives are concerned. Right or wrong, women seem to fare pretty well when they manage their relationships with men in a way that allows the man to think that decisions such as whether to make a commitment or not are totally *his* idea. Dishonest or just good management? Manipulative? Maybe. Effective? Most assuredly.

On the other end of the continuum are the men who are looking to marry their next "mother" and be taken care of their entire life. Still, even these mama's boys sometimes like to think they are running the show.

Bottom line: FACT. Men like to at least feel that they have some control over the course and progress of their relationships.

7. Men think it's weak to acknowledge needs.

Since men have been socialized to be the leaders and providers in relationships, needs just don't fit into the picture. Of course for a man who has been raised to believe that "weak" is figuratively as well as literally a four-letter word, every effort would be made to hide, avoid or deny any deficiency, void or shortcoming that might require help or support from a woman. Again, this is a generality, as some men are ridiculously needy, but for the most part men are not psychologically minded or comfortable acknowledging an emotional need.

The truth is that men do have needs and they know it. Getting them to acknowledge this is a whole other story, however, and that can become a problem for you, because the quality of a relationship depends on the extent to which it meets the needs of the two people involved. In order for you to effectively meet the needs of the man in your life, you first have to know what they are. It is much easier for you to learn what his needs are if he knows them and is willing to share them with you. However, if he doesn't admit that he has needs, he won't know what they are or how to communicate them to you. And therein lies the problem.

Bottom line: FACT. Men don't like to acknowledge their needs and will feel secure doing so only if they know that you will not judge them for being honest.

8. Men want only what they can't have.

I think old sayings get to be old sayings because they are profound. "The grass is always greener on the other side of the fence" was probably said by a guy. Like animals, men are very territorial and very competitive. How does this translate into relationship behavior? Many men do have "roving eyes." This does not mean that they are all infidels who will betray their wives or girlfriends the next time some good-looking or interesting woman crosses their path, but it does mean that many men think about and fantasize about the other side of the fence—if only in passing.

Another way this factor affects relationships is that men will express much more interest in a woman who they cannot take for granted. Territoriality and competitiveness will often kick in if another man begins to show interest in a woman they may have previously lost interest in. It is sometimes as basic as "I don't want her unless you do."

It's beyond stupid and childish, but sometimes the case nonetheless.

Bottom line: FACT—sort of. Men are capable of serious commitment, but do sometimes respond to competitive territorial protection like an alpha male trying to dominate the herd.

---

9. Men are intimidated by strong women.

As it turns out, this may not just be an excuse that women use to explain why they're still single or why they don't get asked out as much as they should. The truth is that powerful, successful women can be terrifying to an insecure man. Like I said, men like to chase. And one of their methods is to figure out what you need and then give it to you. Men like to be the hero, the rescuer, the knight in shining armor. Men like to feel needed, and in fact indispensable, because they believe this puts them in a position of control and security. If he looks at you and sees that you have a solid job, financial security, interesting hobbies and a great social life, he wonders what he has to offer you. When he can't come up with a good enough answer, the intimidation factor sets in—he fears that you won't want him.

Men want to feel needed, especially for their ability to fix things; if he doesn't see how he fits in as a fixer, then he sees no reason for his existence in the relationship.

Strong women who give off the message that a man is merely a convenience for their pleasure often find their men going off to be with women who actually have some needs. It is not so much that a man doesn't like strong women—because men in general prefer independent, smart, energetic, vigorous and participative women—but when a woman's strength trumps his whole reason for being, he would rather find someone who really needs him.

Bottom line: FACT. Men need to clearly perceive why they are needed.

---

10. Men are selfish.

This may be a hard pill to swallow, but it should explain some of the disagreements you may have had in previous relationships: Many men do put their own needs first.

Designed as protectors, men evolved in such a way as to ensure that they were strong so they could deal with procuring food, building lodging and combating threats to safety. It was a matter of basic survival. The male survival instinct has persisted and differs sharply from the female nurturing instinct precisely because males and females are built for such different tasks.

However, whether true altruism actually exists has been a hotly debated question for quite some time. While many people do not consider it to be an admirable trait, most people do enter any situation considering, "What's in this for me?" I suppose this is selfish, but it is grounded in deeply entrenched survival instincts. I'm not offering this to explain away jerky, insensitive and inconsiderate behavior. I am just explaining that while men will provide many profound examples of selfishness, they do not have a corner on the me-first market and, at least in part, have come by their selfishness somewhat honestly. I say "somewhat" because obviously the hope is that as people mature, they develop sensitivity for the wants and needs of others. The good news is that even selfish guys are trainable. You just have to get their attention, understand what motivates them and jerk on their tail every time they do something stupidly selfish.

Bottom line: FACT. Men can be sort of selfish, but so can women, and both can change.

Lost In Translation

Here's a lighthearted and funny look at what men say to women. And sometimes, they're dead on.

Men and women speak different languages. As a psychologist, and someone who has studied male-female relationships for thirty years, I never cease to be amazed at how a woman sometimes fails to "get" obvious messages from some guy who is trying to tell her something. The problem is not that women are negative, picking at their mate's language all the time, but that an awful lot of women seem to be really naive. Many women simply don't pick up on the bright red flares a man sends to indicate that he is losing interest, or to imply what he really wants or to betray impure motives. I continually marvel at how a woman in love can filter out messages that no one else on earth could miss.

There's a world of difference between what a guy may say to a woman and what he really means. To get some clarity and maybe get a few good laughs, look at the following examples translating male-speak:

He said:	*He meant:*
Another glass of wine?	Drink up. We'll both look better.
I need space.	We are so over that I am thinking of going into the witness protection program to get away from you.

You're beautiful.	Thanks for not wearing a bra.
I'll call you.	Good-bye.
Is that a new dress?	Great, how much did that cost me?
I love you.	I want to have sex.
I love you too.	Now can we have sex?
I'm going out with the guys.	If Dave had breasts, I'd never see you again.
I've just been really busy with work.	I'd rather take a beating than spend another hour with you.

But we just spoke two days ago.	How can I miss you if you won't go away?
Let's split the bill.	I'm a cheap bastard.
It's not you, it's me.	It is definitely you.
Sure we can just be friends.	As long as we can do it naked
Can I help with dinner?	Will it ever be ready?
Have you lost weight?	I just booked a golf game for Saturday.
It would take too long to explain.	I have no idea how it works.

How many times have you looked at a man you've dated, shaken your head and wondered, "Can he really be that stupid, insensitive, tuned-out, selfish or clueless?" The answer is, "No, he's probably not that bad." But he is, shall we say, male—as in, action-oriented, protective, goal-directed, strength-preserving. What I'm trying to say is that before you can judge the men in your life you will have to figure out what drives them and why.

As we saw with the facts and fiction, some of the behaviors that cause you to question their mental or emotional skills are pretty easy to explain. Once you understand the reason behind the action, you will have the ultimate edge and be in a position to get more of what you want and less of what you don't want from your target mate. After you've had a chance to review the basics, you'll be amazed that you hadn't put the pieces together sooner.

I mean, honestly, a man can be as predictable and reliable as your SUV; you just have to know how to drive him. You turn the wheel and he goes one way. You push the pedal to the metal and he charges straight ahead. If you're pressing pedals and turning the wheel at random, the responses will seem senseless. But if you manage to figure out how he works, your relationship can go from zero to sixty in no time.

We tested what you think you know about men; now let me fill in some gaps and tell you some things you definitely need to know. Men do have some common traits and tendencies that once understood can give you a tremendous edge in dealing with "the other side." Understand—I am not saying that these things are good or bad. I am just saying that they "are."

My son Jay loves to fish, but growing up he used to complain about having to get up so early in the morning to have a chance of catching anything. I always told him, "Sorry, but fish behave in certain ways and if you want to catch a fish, you have to know what they like, what they do, when they do it and how they do it. If you want to get a fish in the boat, you have to understand fish and use that info to be in the right place at the right time with the right stuff." Hmmm . . . Does that story have any meaning for you, or is it just an anecdote about a boy learning to fish?

I am now going to give you some seldom if ever talked-about scoops on men and their tendency to be:

1. *One-trick ponies*
2. *Clark Kents*
3. *Caveman competitors*
4. *Needy Neds*
5. *Sex gods*
6. *Gordon Gekkos*
7. *Efficiency experts*
8. *Human minefields*

9. *Lifelong pupils*
10. *Sore losers*

Most guys exhibit aspects of all or most of these categories, to varying degrees. If you think some of these behavior types seem to contradict each other, you're right, they do. But like you, men are full of conflicting impulses and needs. These contradictions can be confusing, but they're also part of what makes men fun. These broad categories of how guys act will help you understand the guy in question, and figure out how to fish at the right time with the right equipment.

1. One-Trick Ponies

What It Is: Most men are linear thinkers. They take a single-file, one-thing-at-a-time approach to life. Think of this quality as nature's way of helping men focus singularly on the matter at hand—be it the hunt, the job, the sexual conquest or *Monday Night Football*—without interference. Clearly, this characteristic is not without its pros and cons. As I said, I'm not here to defend it; I am here only to report it. If you are the one thing that a man is currently passionately focused on, obviously that's great. But if at any given point in time you temporarily drop to number four, five or six, you're going to be really frustrated because you're likely to feel rejected, undervalued and hurt.

This is not a totally all-or-nothing phenomenon. He *can* multitask on a bunch of mindless or dispassionate "duties," but when a man's attention has been captivated by something, everything else is going to fade in a hurry. If you catch him when he is already passionately invested in some activity, project or subject matter, and you're trying to talk to him after he has been sucked in, you're wasting your time and talking to yourself. You have to understand this characteristic and realize that you need to get him unplugged from what he was doing and replugged into what you're doing. Otherwise you're likely to get your feelings hurt and walk off in a funk long before you get him unplugged and replugged.

It's called "compartmentalizing." When a man has been previously captivated, he will not hear a word you say, won't think to call or take time out to plan a romantic evening. That is not a good thing for your feelings but it does not mean he doesn't care about you. It doesn't even mean that he prefers the television's company to yours, or that he would rather be working, or that he thinks you're not worth his attention. It can simply mean he is a guy who got caught up in something before you hit the radar screen. Men can tune out plenty of static and focus once they get hooked.

One woman thought her husband had lost all interest in her, that the sizzle had gone and the spark was dead. But they were great friends he really loved her, and she really loved him. She read *Relationship Rescue,* which says it takes only one person in the relationship to make a major change, and decided that on Sunday, the day they both had off, she would reignite the spark with a French maid outfit. So she gets all dressed up and goes into the den where he is watching football. She starts dusting bookshelves, bending over in her French maid's outfit and then gets down to do a striptease. Well, her husband was leaning so far to the left to see around her that he was about to fall out of his Barcalounger. So she writes in to the show and says, "That's it. I guess I just don't have it anymore."

My point is that it's all about compartmentalization. They live in Chicago, so I asked him who had been playing that Sunday. And he said, "The Bears! Who else?" And I asked, "At what point during the game did she come in in her outfit?" And he said "Late fourth quarter. Three points behind. What else?" I said, "What would have happened if she had come in after the game?" "Oh, we'd have done some dusting but by the time the game was over she had gone away mad with her feelings hurt." He was passionately invested in the game at the time, and she came in and wanted him to click off the game that *he had two and a half hours and twenty years of history* invested in. She chose that fifteen minutes to do a striptease. Now that's not a smart move for her or for him. It's all about finding a time when his focus is on you and you only. So we decided to do a follow-up, and they're doing great because now she gets it: Pick your time, pick your battles, everything's fine.

What It Means to You: If you've ever dated a man who seems to forget that telephones exist in other cities, then you know what I'm talking about. And if you've ever dated a man you met while on vacation, forget about it. On vacation, he has nothing to focus on but you and the idea of romance. The second they return to their regularly scheduled programs, however, guys will start backpedaling and you'll be left to wonder, What happened? He was so wonderful those four days in Belize! So, yes, compartments can be helpful, but they can also be hurtful if you don't understand them.

How You Can Use It: If timing is working against you, the best way for you to use this information is simply to stop taking a man's lack of attention so personally. The fact that a man is acting inattentive doesn't mean that he is losing interest in you—or that he has ADD or is a lazy bum. I know women who have told me that the second a guy pulls away even a little bit, the second he immerses himself in work for a while—even if he just rolls over to the other side of the bed—they start freaking out and thinking, "That's it. He doesn't love me. This is the beginning of the end." The truth is that he has just switched his focus for a while to work—to sleep—to attend to the rest of his life.

I repeat: If you want to use this information to your advantage, you need to realize that timing is everything. Pick your times and don't freak when you are not his primary target.

2. Clark Kents

What It Is: Inside a lot of guys there lives a would-be Superman, who can save the day, the planet *and* you, all at a moment's notice. Men are natural problem solvers—or at least that's what they think they are. So when it comes to relationships, you need to understand that men have to feel like heroes. They need to feel as though they are vitally involved, have something to offer and are in a position of power in the relationship. That doesn't mean they have to be the "boss" or that you have to bat your eyes and pretend to be helpless. But you do have to let a man know he has something vital to offer. There is nothing men love more than being needed for their particular skills, whether that means hooking up your stereo equipment, moving your couch, setting up your computer or, more important, being your companion to chase away the loneliness and put a smile on your face.

I played football in high school, and in my senior year I was recruited by a number of schools, including the University of Tulsa. Now a lot of the schools I looked at were much bigger and higher-profile than Tulsa, but I was a receiver and I knew going in that a lot of those bigger schools *ran* the ball all the time while Tulsa *threw* the ball more than anybody in the nation. Sure, Tulsa was a smaller school, but I had something to offer it. I thought, If I go to Tulsa I can have a huge impact. I am the kind of horse they're going to ride. If I go to some "three yards and a cloud of dust" run-oriented school, I could be irrelevant. So where did I go? I went where I felt I had something to offer. Go Tulsa Hurricanes!

What It Means to You: The same logic applies to the guys you date. They need to know how they can contribute to your life. They may look at you and say, "Why would she be interested in me? She's got education, money, social connections. What do I have to offer?" If they think the answer is "nothing, zip, zero, nada," some otherwise good-quality guys might be intimidated and may just pass up a good thing. This is the nuts and bolts of why some men seem to be intimidated by competent women.

You might be thinking, "Hey, that's his problem. If he is that weak, then I don't want him anyway. I am who I am and I'm not going to 'dumb it down' to make him feel macho!" Good point, but what we may have here is a breakdown in communication. Everybody likes to feel wanted, and he might just be worth going to the trouble to point out that even though many parts of your life are working really well, this doesn't mean that you don't have unmet wants and needs just like everybody else.

How You Can Use It: As a competent, self-reliant woman you need to be able to show men that having your act together doesn't mean you don't need them. And that doesn't mean playing a swooning, submissive weakling. Not at all. The trick to working a guy's Clark Kent side is to show him that while you may not need him to rescue you, you still have some wants and desires that only a dedicated, romantic partner can fulfill. To the extent that you can make him feel like your "companionship Superman," he's going to be a happy guy. Later, in Chapter 7, we will go into the art of being a strong, competent, independent woman, while still communicating the fact that you are vulnerable and have needs that the man can meet in the emotional arena.

---

3. Caveman Competitors

What It Is: The thing you have to understand about men is that because they are pretty competitive as a general rule, they tend to be somewhat externally defined. In other words, at least some part of their personal satisfaction comes from comparing themselves to other guys—what other guys have, what other guys want and what other guys do. For men, life is sometimes primarily about competing and winning, not getting hugs, being supported and listened to, although at some level men want and need those things as well. Men are big on staking out their territory, proving their manhood and being strong in the face of challenge.

That's a good thing if your man is in fact competent and you enjoy being taken care of and protected. It's a bad thing if he is an insecure doofus who grew up comparing genital size on the playground and now maintains his ego by always having to drive the big expensive car, wearing the watch he can't afford or tearing muscles trying to be the man on the softball team. If he has children, this is the guy who will try to live through them vicariously as they get into sports or the school play. These are all negative sides of his cavemanness, to be sure, but as I said, it can be productive as well.

Not that men are dogs, but, by way of comparison, you have probably noticed that your dog's behavior changes when another dog comes around. There can be a bone that has been lying in the yard unnoticed for days. Your dog won't even give it a second thought until another dog starts sniffing at it. Then he will fight to the death to protect and keep that bone. That is a perfect example of the caveman mentality, especially when it comes to relationships—and ladies, this is a handy little piece of information to keep in mind, I can assure you.

What It Means to You: If you feel a man is beginning to entertain some doubts about you, there's nothing like a little healthy competition to get him to stop looking at you like chopped liver and start seeing you for the filet mignon that you and all your friends know you are. If somebody he respects, like a friend or social rival, starts showing interest in you and he sees you two hitting it off and having yourselves a great time, your stock and his investment in you will go way up. It is just that plain and simple. If that sounds manipulative and is offensive to your sensibilities, then don't do it. But if you want to win, then you have to understand that men are externally influenced. What they think they want can be externally validated by other guys showing interest, and that may just be the *reminder* he needs that you are absolute gold. Dumb? Maybe, but I'm just telling you how it works.

Also, realize men like to have what I call "sweat equity." If they haven't worked hard to get their position in the relationship, they won't value it. As soon as they think "I've got this locked," this relationship is over and done—it has lost its sizzle, and you will be out the door. As soon as he thinks, "I own her and she is totally committed to me," you can start kissing him good-bye because the clock on your relationship is ticking.

How You Can Use It: Since men are primarily wired to compete with other men, competition also activates the possessive function. When you want to move to the "exclusive" stage or when you are getting ready to close the deal and hear that marriage proposal, you may find an opportunity to use this knowledge to motivate him and keep him focused. This is not about flirting and trying to make your man jealous. It's really more subtle than that. The competition doesn't even have to be another man. If he respects his sister, his mother, his pastor or even his female trainer, and they show interest in you and validate you by getting involved with you on a social level, that is meaningful information to him. It tells him he is barking up the right tree. Believe me, the second he sees someone else interested in you, he will get up on his hind legs and start protecting his territory. And what's more, if he recognizes that you are desirable to others of his breed, he'll feel that you've been approved, and this feeling will stick with him forever.

Also, once you understand this aspect of men, you will know that it doesn't pay to be a pushover. You cannot be his beck-and-call girl. When he does compartmentalize the way I described in "One-Trick Ponies" and cycles away from you for a day, week or month, you have to make sure that he has to earn his way back in the door.

You've got to be a little bit of a mystery, unpredictable as to whether or not you are there. You need to have your own extracurriculars, or be passionate about your work, or have something else that interests you besides your relationship, so that he sometimes has to fight for your attention.

If you don't make him work for it, if you don't make him feel that he is earning his position every step of the way, I promise you it's sweet poison. He might just totally buy into the unconditional acceptance at first, and you'll be riding high, thinking you've got this man all wrapped up; but take my word, if he thinks you worship at the altar of him, he will absolutely start taking you for granted and lose interest. So for the sake of your future, make him understand that he needs to compete for time on your schedule. If he knows you're waiting by the phone and can be ready for him with five minutes' notice, then he's always going to call you five minutes before a date.

4. Needy Neds

What It Is: As I described in the "Caveman" section, men live in a world they often define as a highly competitive, dog-eat-dog, scorekeeping environment. They need validation from their friends, their colleagues, their families—but the validation from the woman they love is the kind they value the most. When a guy comes home, he wants and needs to be accepted and to feel that the woman in his life is proud of the way he works, fathers, looks and so forth. It's his catnip. But he will seldom ask for praise and may not even consciously recognize that it is highly important to his feelings of self-worth and well-being.

The fact that he has needs is, of course, actually a good thing and certainly not anything for him to be ashamed of or upset about. Identifying the priorities within his needs system can be an important thing for you to do in developing a relationship. The problem is that men often lack insight into their needs, and therefore have a difficult time articulating them or even so much as admitting that they exist. On the other hand, there are men who are so needy, so whiny, that meeting their needs is like trying to fill a bottomless pit. You want to be needed, but you do not want to be sucked dry.

What It Means to You: You and I both know that needs are nothing to be ashamed of, but don't try to tell that to most guys. Men don't talk about needs, because, as I said, deep down most men believe they are weaknesses. So it's hard for women to know what a man's needs are. Because men can't or won't talk about them, much of your job is to go on a quest to discover what your man's most prominent needs are. Once you identify these needs and see that they are relatively healthy, your goal is to figure out a way to meet them.

How You Can Use It: If you know what a man needs and you give it to him (because you have decided it is healthy for both of you to do so), his experience of you will be of high quality. He will be drawn to you, he will seek you out and he will soak up the validation that you have to offer. The more he falls in love with you, the greater power you have to validate him and the more he will value you for his balance in the world. The boys' club may not applaud men for their family skills, but you can. And you should.

Men need to know that they cause you to feel safe and secure, that you trust their ability to partner with you. They need to know that you find them attractive and are proud to be seen with them. This of course presupposes that you do in fact feel this way about them. If you do not, then you are with the wrong man.

Every man needs to feel a sense of acceptance and a strong sense of belonging to someone. If you provide that for him, if you become his "soft place to fall," you will become a vital part of his life and his future. Your man may not be the president of the United States, he may not be stamping out disease and suffering or curing the social ills of the world, but what he does will be important to him—and if he knows it is respected by you, a person whom he values greatly, then he will be one grateful guy.

5. Sex Gods

What It Is: Did I mention that sex is really important to men? Well, let me say it again because it cannot be stressed enough. Men need to feel sexually powerful. When my dad was alive, he used to give a lot of speeches of a psychological nature; and I often heard him say that a man doesn't really want to have sex constantly—what he wants is to feel that he will be accepted by the woman in his life (and that she will constantly tell him how good he is at having sex!). It is a rare man who can admit that given the opportunity, he would not be having sex 24/7. Sure, he can go all day, all night and then some. Of course he can have sex eight days a week, three times a day if that's what you want. He is a sexual animal. Hear him roar! And if you believe all that, I've got some great beachfront property to show you in Arizona! Certainly men have different levels of sex drives, with some being more motivated than others, but for the most part, men talk a lot bigger game than they deliver.

What It Means to You: Men need to feel virile and attractive. Some men are actually even quite romantic. But either way, as we talked about earlier in this chapter, men need to feel strong and accepted. That is why, at least in part, many women report that they will fake an orgasm rather than deal with the insecurity and hurt feelings that come when he doesn't get affirming feedback. The old pat on the shoulder would just break his heart after all the hard work he put in. It's as if you're pulling him out of the game because of poor performance. Many women just don't have the stomach for it. Given men's goal-oriented nature, if they can't please you, they feel like failures.

How You Can Use It: Once you have done your homework and identified your man's needs, and made the value judgment that those needs are healthy and things you can feel good about meeting, it is time to make a very focused "to do" list. Once his needs are identified, and you make them a priority, you are going to be building power regarding your ability to bond with this man and solidify a committed relationship. If you are already in a relationship, and it seems to be losing its sizzle, this is a good way to rekindle it. If you have sex with your man and you enjoy it, tell him how amazing it was. That is absolute music to his ears. He will be so excited by the sound of your sincere praise and appreciation that he will keep coming back for more. Of course, this isn't to say that you should lie and fake orgasms if you are having a horrible time. If that's the case, it may be time to put your teacher's hat on and start giving lessons.

Making your needs known can also be a powerful bonding tool. If you teach him what your needs are and you motivate him to meet them, he will feel vital and empowered and therefore comfortable in the relationship. This is major power! Embrace it and you can drive the relationship to the level of intensity you want.

---

6. Gordon Gekkos

What It Is: "Greed works" is much more than a popular line from a classic Oliver Stone movie; it is a fact of life. As I mentioned earlier, when approaching any situation, everyone thinks, "What's in it for me?" Men never waste their time doing something for nothing. Men tend to be scorekeepers and are always looking for a payoff—whether that's a good time, money or the avoidance of uncomfortable emotions such as guilt, men need a recognizable payoff. If they get it, they will come back for more. If they don't, they won't. It is that simple.

What It Means to You: Don't judge a man's greed—use it to your advantage. Understand the hydraulics of reinforcement psychology. Behaviors that are followed by a reward tend to recur. Behaviors that are not followed by a reward tend not to recur.

If you want him to keep paying attention to you, then you need to pay him in some way for doing that. On the other hand, if you teach a guy that no matter what he does, he is going to get the same response out of you, he will never be able to figure out what it is you want him to do.

How You Can Use It: You can appeal to a guy's graciousness, his altruism, his sense of fair play, but nothing will be as powerful as appealing to his greed. If you can see things through his eyes and understand what he at least thinks he wants, you can really target your responses. By understanding that he approaches a situation from the standpoint of "what's in this for me" and by choosing to respond in a way that gives a clear and relevant answer to that question, you are going to be really effective in shaping and directing his behavior. I'm not saying that you should do that if it is unhealthy for you or for him; but giving him what he wants, or even just presenting what you're going to do in such a way that it addresses what he thinks he wants, will be very powerful. If some of his behaviors are rewarded and others are not, you will begin to shape his behavior, emotions and priorities. We will talk more about how to execute these moves in Chapter 7.

7. Efficiency Experts

What It Is: Trust me, men are not as tuned out as they sometimes seem. Sure, they may be horrible at remembering anniversaries, but that's only because their priorities may be completely different from yours. It has long been said that a man's going to do what he wants to do most. A man's goal is typically to get everything done—as quickly as possible, so he can get more stuff done. That's why so many guys are speed freaks, driving their cars way over the limit and bragging about how fast they made it from Moline to Peoria, expecting everyone else to hang in there like camels. They're the men who go around saying, "We're crazy busy, but that's how we like it."

The term "man of action" did not come out of a vacuum—men are basically happiest when they're busy. Maybe it's because they can't bear children and you need only one man for every hundred women or so to ensure the survival of the species, but men have a deep-seated desire to feel necessary, important and purposeful—and that translates into being productive and active.

What It Means to You: Spreading themselves thin means that their schedules are often at odds with yours. Don't get me wrong—most of the women I know are extremely busy and keep more balls in the air than any man could even conceive of. It is the combination of different priorities and "compartmentalized" busyness that gets a man into trouble every time. Men simply do not put the same things at the top of their priorities lists as women do. Men invariably underestimate the importance of certain things to women, and if you combine that miscalculation with the fact that they are focused on what they actually believe is important, what you wind up with is a man in the doghouse!

Here's a painful example: It's not at all unusual that when I'm about to go out for the evening, I race in at the last minute from a previously scheduled meeting (read that as tennis game). I jump into the shower while Robin looks on, wondering how in the world I am ever going to make it. In a couple of minutes, I have jumped out of the shower, have shaken myself like a dog and am throwing on my clothes and getting ready to head out the door. I am fast. It's not like I have to do my hair! At every step of the way, I am staying clearly focused on the efficiency with which I achieve each task. While the shower is warming up, I am stacking socks, underwear, shoes, shirts, pants, billfold, watch and the ever important wedding ring all in a convenient place to cut down on steps. I am focused, I am efficient . . . I am in trouble; I just don't know it yet. Once I am through, and only once I am through, will I settle down, take a deep breath and realize that Robin has spent two and a half hours getting ready, and was waiting for me to react to how she looked as soon as I came in the door. It may have been fifteen minutes since I ran into the house and saw her, but only now am I ready to tell her how great she looks. Too late—I'm toast!

How You Can Use It: Don't get mad. Express yourself. You have to figure out what is important to you and then actively set up your world to ensure that your priorities get met. The fact is that you have to actually tell men what you want and you have to tell them often. I'm not saying men are dumb, but sometimes you have to wonder, watching what they do and don't do. I know, I know, you probably think that if they didn't realize it on their own, if you had to bring it up, then it's not important to them. And if they don't care, then what's the point? Here is the point: It may not feel as good to tell a guy that you love getting flowers or that you want to do something ridiculously romantic on Valentine's Day, but if you want something bad enough, you'll need to tell your guy as much, because the last thing he'll be able to do is read your facial expression while he's watching *SportsCenter*.

Should you *have* to tell him, over and over again? No. But that's just how it is. I'm not defending it, just describing it. Recognizing this quality and knowing how to deal with it can save a lot of frustration and increase your efficiency in building a harmonious relationship. Can he ultimately be trained so you don't have to spoon-feed him over and over? For some men the answer is yes, but for others you just may have to pin a note to their shirt every day leading up to your anniversary—and while you're at it, include some pictures. Pictures are good.

What It Is: Every person has certain unspoken priorities, sensitivities, fears, needs, wants and desires. Men are no different. All men have a history, and there are certain things based on that history that they are going to bring to any relationship. It is typically referred to as baggage, but that has a negative connotation. History can be positive as well as negative.

Anyone who is in a relationship is either contributing to building or contaminating that relationship every hour of every day. If the man you are focused on has had a difficult and painful history and has done nothing to heal those wounds, chances are he is going to be contaminating his relationship with you.

The pain he brings to the relationship may have to do with prior romantic entanglements or it may not. Maybe he has been working to move up the corporate ladder and watched bitterly as others passed him by. Maybe he had bad sexual experiences in the past and is insecure about his performance. Or it could be that he didn't test well and blew the SATs in high school, and now he secretly believes that he's dumb. All these things can contribute to his areas of sensitivity. Learning what these sensitivities are and making a realistic assessment of what role they might play can be very important.

What It Means to You: To know what a guy is sensitive about is to have a great amount of power and responsibility. It is this kind of sensitivity, it is this ability to read people and know where the rubber meets the road in another person's life, that makes someone a great "people person." You can be a great people person if you just tune in. If you will just look, listen and learn, people will tell you, show you and demonstrate to you everything that is of importance to them. If they don't tell you in so many words, they may let you know by avoiding a particular subject like the bird flu. They will behave in ways that reveal their positions. Once you know your target guy's secret hopes, fears and needs, you have tremendous power that can be used or misused. You can push his buttons and manipulate him into anything, or you can use your power as a guide to being a responsive and relevant companion. With power comes responsibility.

How You Can Use It: You have to understand that your knowledge of a guy's hot buttons can backfire on you if you ever try to use this information against him. It will feel like a betrayal to him, and he may not be able to forgive you. The way to make the most out of the human minefield aspect is to recognize what needs are triggered by those areas of sensitivity and commit to healthfully meeting those needs. If you provide much-needed support for those highly sensitive areas, your "stock" will go through the roof. If you are sincere, then you're just loving smart; if you are insincere, the relationship will be in the ditch in no time.

9. Lifelong Pupils

What It Is: It's been my long-held belief that we teach people how to treat us. I know you've heard that men don't change. Nonsense. Men can change like anyone else. But change isn't easy, and it takes effort. And as I've implied numerous times, if a regular guy woke up to find a couch tied to his back and a remote control glued to his hand, he'd think he died and went to heaven. Unless, of course, the television was less than thirty-two inches and stuck on the Food Channel—in which case, it might feel more like hell. My point is that men are not too keen on expending more effort than necessary, especially not in the relationship department. Like all people, men like to do what they're good at, and that doesn't usually include relationships. I was never good at math in school, and therefore it was a subject in which I needed a lot of practice. But I absolutely hated to work on math, because it just didn't come easy. It wasn't natural. Same thing with men and understanding emotions—it just doesn't come as naturally for men as it is does for women, so it can feel like a job, a scary job. If something feels like work, they will rebel against it.

What It Means to You: Men are hard, but not impossible to train, not because they're not smart, but just because this is not their long suit or their priority. But lecturing is out of the question. Life with a man can be a constant game of show-and-tell. If a man cares about you, he is definitely going to want you to be happy. You can shape his behavior by making a clear connection between the things he does and the reactions you have. Give him positive feedback. Pouting seldom works, because, frankly, it's too subtle. When it comes to emotions I've often said that men need the dots put really close together and then connected with a bright red line. Anything is easy when you know how it's done, and most women know how to deal with emotions, express emotions and even feel emotions a lot better than most men. You can be his guide, but you'll need a great deal of patience.

How You Can Use It: A lot of women will walk away from a guy because they become frustrated with his seeming insensitivity. This is understandable, because there are some men who need a lot less training than other men. If you want to hold out for one of those "sensitive types," then more power to you. But you might be able to train the one you have into being what you want and need on the emotional front in less time than it takes to find one who's already there. Don't take yourself out of the game too quickly if a lot of other traits and characteristics are on target.

10. Sore Losers

What It Is: No one likes to lose, but men really, really can't stand it! Because of their competitive nature, power and control are extremely important in their self-perceptions. Sure, there are some guys who quit the rat race and go join a commune in the mountains somewhere. But even then I bet they work to make it the "best" commune ever! Men are socialized to measure value in terms of how much power, control, money, recognition and even material things they accumulate—not how sensitive they can be or how deeply they can connect with another person.

When men lose a battle, they take it personally because to them, it's not just a matter of losing but a test of wills, a test of manhood and worth. Whereas a woman can lose a chess match or a volleyball game and still feel great about herself, a man is more likely to take losing as a blow to his ego.

Men may feel like they lost a fight and have been shown to be weaker. If they get a bad score in golf, even though golf may have no relevance to their life, the loss will stay with them for the rest of the week. This explains why there are so many more men playing golf than women—they're out there trying to get their pride back!

What This Means to You: This is all about you and the male ego. When men take a hit to their pride and ego, they will sulk and pout for days—maybe longer. At all costs, avoid making your guy feel like a loser. This will only ensure that there are no winners in your relationship. This doesn't mean that you have to tiptoe around or handle him with kid gloves, but with people in general, and with men in particular, it makes much better sense to "work the problem," deal with the issues, and not allow yourself to get into personal affronts and character assassination. It comes down to the rules of fighting fair. Personal attacks violate those rules and greatly jeopardize your relationship with any partner.

How You Can Use It: Understanding that power, ego and control are part of his internal need system, choose your battles wisely. Don't fight to always be right and lose sight of his needs. A smart woman knows how to help a man maintain his need for power and control without losing herself. It boils down to being a gracious winner, which is not to be confused with rolling over, and allowing him to strut around and thump his chest when he has been wrong. It's the subtle art that is the best part of being a woman—you can get a view of the entire game board and know that one move doesn't mean the entire game is lost.

What Not to Do

Never use the information you get from a man against him in an argument. To women, intimacy means closeness. To men, it means vulnerability. Relationships in general, and intimacy in particular, are all about taking down your defenses and leaving yourself open. That means trusting people enough to give them the power to emotionally injure you, which is absolutely contrary to a man's nature.

To gain his trust, you must teach him that when he allows himself to be vulnerable with you, it makes you love and respect him more, not less. One huge mistake you can make in a relationship is to take classified information he's given you about himself and to use it as leverage in an argument. If your partner opens up to you about his fears, needs, desires and other secrets, and you turn that on him you've gone to a place from which there is probably no recovery.

Once you've processed all the information in this chapter, I want you to be honest: Do you want your man to really love you, or do you want him to love you the way you would love you? Think about it, because it's an important distinction. If it's the latter, you need to remind yourself that in many ways, you're dealing with a real guy, not some fantasy mate. You can't take his personality personally—he was this way long before you came along. He's not behaving in these ways in order to make your life difficult; he's acting like this because that's how he's been acting for years. Like I said, he can change some things, but he's also his own person, separate from you. If you insist on acting as if you two are the same and pretending that understanding should just come naturally, you're not going to get anywhere.

Now ask yourself:

1. *Am I wanting or expecting the wrong thing?*
2. *Am I failing to recognize that the men I date are giving me what I want?*

3. *Am I asking my dates to give me something they don't have?*
4. *Am I working with these men or against them?*
5. *Am I trying to change these guys to suit my specifications and not accepting them for who they are?*

If you answered yes to any of those questions, part of your solution may be very much under your own control, if you'll just recognize it. Your new question should be: How can I use the information I just learned about men and about myself to create the best relationship I can? How can I interpret a guy's actions so that I am not constantly getting hurt and offended?

Creating the relationship you want starts with understanding the nature of the "beast" you're dealing with. It's important to understand the nature, habits, traits and tendencies so you don't misinterpret or personalize things that are not aimed at you and are not affronts to you, but are simply the nature of who you are dealing with.

This doesn't mean that you have to like his nature or that you don't seek to modify it within reason, but at least understanding it can keep you from getting your feelings hurt needlessly. More harshly put: It isn't always about you. That can be a good thing or a bad thing, but either way, the fact remains—his behavior is not always about you.

Not to keep comparing guys to dogs, but consider for a moment how your dog could hurt your feelings if you didn't understand him. If he turns and leaves every time you give him a treat and you don't realize that he's doing it to protect his treasure and not because he is simply not interested in your company and is rejecting you, you and your puppy might have some seriously strained relations. Once you realize that he's just doing what the good Lord intended him to do, what he has been genetically encoded to do, you can calm down and figure out what to do so you get more of what you want and less of what you don't.

The Dark Side

For all I've said about guys in this chapter, there is something I haven't mentioned. I've known some really bad guys in my time. That's right, what I'm telling you is that you are not crazy—a lot of your worst suspicions are often true. Many guys do have a dark side. I wouldn't be leveling with you if I didn't tell you that there really does exist a certain element that is psychopathic and exploitative. Watch out for these five types:

1. *The hit 'er-and-quit 'er*—*These guys are the ones who just don't like women, yet they use women as often as possible. They still want sex, but their need for intimacy and female companionship ends at the foot of the bed. They will say virtually anything to get a girl naked and have no conscience about what lies and misrepresentations they tell to get there. They are predators and*

will move on, even if they like the woman. Watch out for men who try to pressure you into having sex with over-the-top urgency and get aggressive when you say no.

2. *The kiss-and-teller*—These are the braggarts who are more interested in a trophy for the sole purpose of having a story to tell. Unlike the previous guy, who may not even care about his image, these guys can't wait to parade you around and then get away from you, so they can tell their stories. It's the old rule about a guy's "magic number"—if a man tells you how many people he slept with, divide that number by two to get the real estimate. Then tell him to take a hike. Their only interest is meeting what they believe are society's expectations. So they won't try to get to know you at all. They just want to show you off and make people think that they've got something—even if they don't.

3. *The smother brother*—These guys are overwhelmed by a need for control. If you let them, they will do what they can to take over your entire life. These are the guys who tell a girlfriend how to dress and where she is and is not allowed to go. Their problem is that they cannot deal with uncertainty, and they micromanage the life out of you and the relationship. At first it may feel good that they are really head over heels in love with you and so invested in you. But be patient, because you may soon find that their only interest is not in caring for you, but in controlling you. Don't confuse smothering with love.
4. *The pretender*—He is playing a script and he doesn't care who is playing opposite him. He just likes his role of romantic lead, which he may eagerly play all the way up to the altar. But he has no intention of ever following through by sticking

around to do any of the actual work. Once this guy feels he's got you, it's game over. Now he's got to figure out what to do with you. And that's either too scary or too boring a proposition for him to deal with, so he moves on to the next victim.

5. *The mama's boy*—Unemployed and seeking women who are affluent to take care of them emotionally and financially, mama's boys are looking to be, you guessed it, mommied. Instead of viewing relationships as their chance to grow into adulthood, they look at women as mothers who will feed, clothe and clean up after them. Watch out for guys who never seem to have any money, expecting you to pay for dinner and asking for loans.

Boy, oh boy, can I put some faces with each of those five categories. These guys are out there. Beware.

7

Your Man Plan

To attract men I wear a perfume called New Car Interior.

RITA RUDNER

At this point, you've gotten in touch with your inner bride. You've figured out what you want in a future husband. And you've got a clue about why you're still single when friends around you are pairing up like the animals on the ark. So now it's time to go shopping for Mr. Right. Instead of viewing yourself as a hunter bounding toward the man of your dreams, shift your point of view and think of yourself as a magnet pulling him *to* you. As with many things in life, the best way to do this is with a strategy. Meeting the love of your life doesn't take one huge step; it takes lots of little steps in the right direction. Here's where we'll talk about your strategy for making all the right moves to get what you want.

Step 1: Getting In

It sounds like a cliché, but your Mr. Right can't fall in love with you if you're sitting at home alone in your pjs and fuzzy slippers cuddling up to a pint of Ben & Jerry's. The story of Rapunzel is called a *fairy tale* for a reason. It's completely unrealistic. Your man isn't going to fight dragons, swim through shark-infested waters and climb through thorny bushes to bust you out of your living room. While you may always be a princess to your mom and dad, you can't expect any guy to think of you that way when other women are so much easier to reach. The first step to finding your perfect counterpart is to get out of the house. Embrace quantity—success may boil down to math, not magic. Old sayings stand the test of time because they are true. You can't get a hit if you're not swinging, you can't get a bite if you don't have your hook in the water and you can't get wet if you don't get in the water. Even though I don't know you personally, one thing I'm sure of is that "the one" isn't going to come knocking on your door or materialize on your couch. Love isn't the pizza man; it doesn't deliver.

So this is the part of the book where I tell you jack it up and get in the game. To up your chance of finding him you've got to get out there, make an effort and make sure you see and are seen by as many qualified new guys as possible. Dating is a numbers game. The more men you meet, the more likely you will find your special someone. So get out there. If you're wondering, "Get out there? Get out where?" here are some ideas:

Right place, right time—Now that you've got a rough sketch of the Character of Him from your work in Chapter 2, think about where that kind of guy would hang out. I call this a "target-rich environment." In other words, a place teeming with the kind of men you're after. You're not going to go hunting for elephants in a rabbit patch, so why would you go looking for investment bankers at a monster truck rally? You don't have to be an heiress or a socialite to meet and marry someone who is successful and capable of providing for you and your family. But you do have to be in the right place at the right time. How do you do that? You go where these guys hang out. If you're looking for the professional type, go to spots where young executives congregate, like parks in and around your town's financial district or hot lunch spots. Can't afford the food? That's no excuse. Just get a cup of coffee, a glass of wine or an appetizer.

You need to get out of your comfort zone—to expand your pool of potentials, don't stick with just one dating locale. Many women lose at the dating game because they go to the same-old spots all the time. I know those places feel safe and give you a certain comfort level whereas going somewhere new can make you feel anxious or insecure. But this isn't *Cheers*. You don't want to go somewhere where everybody knows your name. (Besides, Cliff's a blowhard who lives with his mom, Norm's a married alcoholic and Sam's a womanizer.) You want to go to new places and see new faces. If you go to the same coffee shop or club every weekend, you already know most of the men there and they know you. By now, you should realize that your ordinary hangout isn't the place to meet extraordinary men. If it were, would you still be single? This doesn't mean you should ignore safety. Always be safe, but broaden your horizon.

I'm not saying you can't still go to those old favorite places; I'm just saying you should expand your repertoire. Go to different kinds of places. If you go only to places in the same category—like always going to bars or to bookstores—then you're always going to meet the same type of people. Mix it up and give yourself more variety to choose from. Go to a hip new restaurant in town one night and an art gallery opening the next. Head to the park with your pooch on Saturday and hit the gym on Sunday. Go to church or temple functions. Go bowling one day and on a wine-tasting tour the next. Up the number of different venues you hit, because then you'll see a new crop of faces and they'll see you.

Now when I say go where the men are, I don't mean at the expense of your own good time. You have to make sure it's something you're interested in too. Go to places you'd enjoy even if you weren't looking for the love of your life. If you can't stand sports, don't go to baseball games. If you're not artsy, skip the poetry readings. One woman I know couldn't figure out why she kept going out with guys whose favorite pastime was watching ESPN and never making it past the second date. Then her sister pointed out that she did all her man hunting at sports bars. Who else was she going to meet there? Do things you actually like and you'll make a love connection with someone who has something in common with you.

Resist putting yourself in situations that feel unnatural, because trying to act like someone else is no way to start a relationship. Instead of feigning an interest just to meet a guy, explore your true passions and let the things you really enjoy be the backdrop to your social life. Think about your interests and what's important to you, then find activities to match these interests—whether that means signing up for cooking or art classes, volunteering for a political campaign or a children's charity, working behind the scenes in a theater, attending a work conference or joining a local sports club, you're bound to meet people who share at least one of your priorities. Social groups in your office and community are also good ways to get into a target-rich environment. Think about the stuff your brother, guy pals and male coworkers do in their free time. Then, if it strikes you as something you may be interested in, go ahead and do it yourself.

Here's the thing: As long as you're really into what you're doing, you're going to give off a cool, passionate vibe that makes you seem like the catch of the day.

There's nothing more attractive than a woman who's having fun.

Target-Rich Environments

To get what you want in your future mate, you've got to go where the men are. Of course, no one says you can't meet your husband in line at the DMV or at the nail salon, but those aren't places to actively do your search. The array of locales for meeting men is endless. Here are thirty-one top spots to choose from:

1. *Your church or temple*
2. *Batting cages*
3. *The U.S. Opens (golf and tennis)*
4. *Baseball games*
5. *Major sporting events ranging from the Super Bowl to college or local events*
6. *Sports bars*
7. *Cigar bars*
8. *Sporting goods stores*
9. *Music festivals*
10. *Concerts*
11. *Art galleries*
12. *Car shows*

13. *Golf courses*
14. *Your office*
15. *Clubs*
16. *The bars of trendy restaurants*
17. *The park*
18. *The dog run*
19. *The Internet*
20. *The gym*
21. *Philanthropic groups (e.g., Habitat for Humanity)*
22. *Political campaigns or organizations*
23. *Auto racing events*
24. *Airplanes*
25. *Bookstores*
26. *Tennis courts*
27. *Shooting range*
28. *Starbucks*
29. *Lacrosse games*
30. *Hockey games*
31. *Hardware stores*

Besides mixing up the places you go, mix up the people you go with. Don't always head out in a pack of six girlfriends. I know there's safety in numbers (and you should never go out totally alone, for that reason), but you're not going to get a date as a basketball team. Guys are less likely to come over if they feel they've got an audience. They don't want to get rejected in front of four or five staring women. And with a big group of good friends it's all too easy to get so caught up chatting that you don't pay attention to anyone outside your group. Catching up with your friends is all well and good—during Sunday brunch! But reserve the prime hours for your love life, not your social life. Keep the size of the posse down to one or two friends—a considerably more approachable alternative.

Vary which friends you go out with, too. Often, different people bring out different aspects of our personalities. Maybe one friend brings out your chattier side, so you're more outgoing. Another may be more daring, so she'll get you out on the dance floor or encourage you to introduce yourself to a possible prospect. If you're always going out with married friends or your guy pals, it will look as if you're taken or don't want to be approached. This is the kiss of death in dating—it's just not inviting.

Of course, not all guy friends are bad. One woman I know swears by her best friend, who she says makes an excellent wingman. This woman only needs to tell her friend which guy she finds attractive, and within minutes, she finds not only that her friend has opened up a conversation with this guy's group, but that he's distracted the unsuitable candidate who had been bothering her so that she can freely talk to the guy she'd been eyeing all along. Now that's what I call a real friend.

Step 3: Making Your Approach

Once you've narrowed down where you're going, and who you're bringing along, you have to work on your strategy for meeting men at these places and for how you'll act when you do. Being prepared ensures that you're not flustered or stammering when an interesting guy is nearby. If you know what to reveal about yourself or how to start the conversation, you'll come off confident and self-assured. You'll be less afraid of meeting new people or chatting with someone. One of the things I learned as a pilot is that the most dangerous flying time is when you're taking off and landing. Not much happens at 10,000 or 40,000 feet, but things do happen when you're in close proximity to the ground. That's why we were always taught to get everything done as early as we could so when we were near the ground, all we had to think about was not running into it. Nothing else. That's why a plane's instrument panel has a placard that says "Fire" in plain view and then lists the first five things you should do so that when the engine's burning you don't have to think or look anything up in a manual. All you have to do is what's on the list: cut the fuel, cut the electricity, do this, do that. Same goes for dating. You won't have to come up with your own plan under pressure, because it's all spelled out for you. And that's how prepared I want you to be.

To become the fine-tuned conversationalist we all want you to be, you need only follow these rules:

1. **Know Your Audience**—Part of planning ahead is knowing what the people you're going to be around are interested in so that you're not standing there wondering what the hell everyone else is talking about. If you know the crowd is going to be a bunch of sports fans, like at a Super Bowl party, brush up on some basic and up-to-the-minute sports facts. I'm not saying you need to be a sports maven, but if Shaq was just traded that day, you should know that. If the Yankees won the World Series, you should know that. If you have a professional football team in your city, learn a little bit about it. Read about it in the paper or check out its website.

   I'm not telling you to be somebody you're not, or that all of a sudden you should be doing play-by-play. You don't have to pretend you're interested in football, basketball, NASCAR or anything else to meet a guy. (And you shouldn't, because your lack of interest will just come out later.) But this doesn't mean that you can't be socially sensitive enough to at least know a bit about a topic that's probably of interest to your target group. (By the way, guys don't really think it's cute if a woman says she doesn't know the difference between a touchdown and a home run any more than you'd think it was cute if a guy said he thought Williams-Sonoma was a hot Latino singer.) This way you've got some comments to offer and questions to ask. This isn't being fake. It's just a way to jump-start a conversation or feel comfortable taking part in one. That's often the hardest part, and if you've got an arsenal of topics to get you going, you won't be nervous.

2 **Know Your Opening Questions**—The toughest part of meeting someone is getting the conversation rolling. That's why you've got do a little more homework and come up with five to ten questions you can ask that old boy. One of the most important things I can tell you is that people truly love to be

the focus of attention. They love to be the star. If you spend the whole time talking about yourself, not only will you bore him but it may seem that you're trying way too hard to sell yourself. Give him the attention he craves, on the other hand, and he'll be in a good mood and feel better about you. That's why these five to ten questions will be all about him.

Self-disclosure should be used only 25 percent of the time. The other 75 percent should be listening.

That's an important point. Don't just ask a question and then space out while he's answering or move on to the next question on your list. You'll sound as scripted as a telemarketer. Pay attention, ask follow-up questions and show him you want to know more. Having your five to ten icebreaking questions at the ready keeps you from having to think under pressure or when you're flustered.

If you think conversation should just flow naturally, think again. Barbara Walters, Diane Sawyer, Katie Couric, Julie Chen, Oprah and I interview all kinds of people in our profession and each one of us prepares. A little preparation will go a long way toward reducing your anxiety, because you have a plan. If you ever took a speech class in high school or college, then you know what I am talking about: While you never want to read or memorize your entire presentation, you absolutely must memorize and know your introduction stone-cold. That's what we're doing here. Of course, you can react, ask follow-up questions and play it by ear once you get into the spontaneity of the relationship, but have a solid opening so you know how to begin. When you're prepared like that you're already one step ahead. Nerves won't get the best of you, and you'll feel confident. Here are some basic questions to ask within the first ten minutes of your encounter:

Icebreaking Questions

What's the most fascinating thing about your job?
Do you love what you do for a living or work to pay the bills?
What's your favorite book?
What do you like to do in your free time?
What is your favorite city you have ever lived in?
After an exhausting day at work, what is the first thing you like to do?
Which family member are you closest to?
What was the best concert you've ever been to? (Or even, What was the first concert you ever went to?)
What is your favorite movie?
Do you have any pets?
What's the best vacation you've ever been on? (Are you a mountain person or a beach person?)

The "Deserted Island" Questions

"If you were stranded on a deserted island, and you could have only three of your most prized possessions with you—and sunscreen—what or who would you have?" This is what I call a deserted island question. Maybe you've been asked one or more of these before. And with good reason—they're great conversation pieces.

If you could plan a dinner party, who (alive or dead) would you invite to it?
What are your top five favorite songs of all time?
If you could travel anywhere and you had to leave today, where would you go?
If you could keep only one of your five senses, which one would it be and why?
What would you rather have: two very close best friends or tons of acquaintances?
Do you ever remember your dreams? Do you have any recurring dreams?
What annoys you more than anything else in the world?

If you won $10 million in the lottery, what would you do with the money?

In Chapter 9, when it is time to move on to more probative questions, you will find out what he is made of.

3 **Know Your Star Power**—The secret to star quality is that it is not about hogging the spotlight. On the contrary, the more generous you are about making other people feel like stars, the more star quality you yourself will possess. Asking questions and actually caring enough to listen to the answers is all you need to make people feel special and walk away from your experience feeling good about themselves and you.

There is an interesting story about a woman who was an assistant to a senator. She'd been working very hard on a project, and when a state dinner came up and the senator couldn't go, he gave her his ticket. It was the biggest deal of her life. Friends lent her jewelry. She bought a dress. She got her hair done. She was the first one there and the last to leave. Of course, the next day her buddies wanted to hear all about it. "On one side of me was a well-known ambassador," she said. "He had known every head of state for the last twenty years and regaled me with the most interesting stories. Then another guy came and sat down on the other side and I told him all about you guys." Her friends asked, "So, you like the ambassador the best?" "No," she said. "I liked the other guy better, because after talking to him I felt like I was the most interesting person I have ever met. He asked me about me. He asked what I did, what my parents thought about my job and where I grew up. After I got through talking to him, I thought I was so fascinating. He made me feel special." The moral of this story? If you want to be a star, rise above the noise. If everybody else in the room is saying, "Me, me, me" and you're saying, "You, you,

you" you're the one who's going to get noticed.

4 **Know Your Sound Bite**—Usually when you meet someone new, some typical questions pop up, like "What do you do?" and "Where are you from?" Use the sound bite you prepared for yourself in Chapter 5 so you're never stumped by these very basic queries. Be positive and upbeat in your replies. If you say, "Boy, does my job suck. I hate it," you'll come off like a downer and someone with a negative attitude. People will feel sorry for you and stay away. But if you talk about things with optimism, pride and passion, others will be drawn to you. You may be a secretary and dislike your job intensely, but say something positive about it, like, "I'm in transactions over at the bank. It's a great group of people." If they ask if the job is fun, you can say, "I don't know about whether the work is fun, but the people sure are." You don't have to lie; just give it an upbeat spin. If you do love your job, tell them why. When you talk about where you're

from, don't roll your eyes and tell them how you grew up in a boring hick town. Have an interesting story to tell about your childhood or your hometown.

Part of having a good sound bite is being prepared with a list of four or five things that you think are important for anybody to know about you. Maybe you'll list your job, your hobbies, your religion, your politics or your quirky take on something in the world, but if somebody's going to be interested in you, it's these five things that'll pique his interest and pull him in. Or maybe these things will turn him off—if that's the case, you'd rather know it up front.

5 **Know Your Fillers**—Define four or five things you can talk about at any time to anyone. Then know these topics inside out and make sure you're comfortable with them. These can be saviors when you don't know what to say or when you hit a lull in conversation. Good fillers can be talking about a place where you often vacation, a hobby that you have or an aspect of

your job that's interesting. Some of the best filler topics are based on current events; this is why it's best to stay on top of what's going on, both in the world and in your community.

Before going out, read a newspaper or visit a news website and scan the day's top stories. Or turn on CNN so you can listen to it while you're getting ready. If the housing bubble everyone had been talking about actually burst that day, you ought to know about it. If you live in Los Angeles and the city just elected a new mayor, you should know that, too. Tune in to what's happening in the world, so when someone says, "What do you think about Condoleezza Rice not willing to testify under oath?" you can say something besides, "Huh? Condawhata who?" Of course you know who she is, but you get what I'm saying. Stay current. Not only does this strategy make you look smarter because you're up to speed on breaking news, but it'll give you quick and current conversation starters. Since most people will know something about these topics, it becomes an instant connection.

Granted, the news can be controversial, but you don't have to state an opinion or start a heated debate. Just say something general, like, "Can you believe what's going on in the real-estate market?" If the other person's heard the news, then he can talk about it and give his opinions and comments. If he hasn't, then you seem smart, hip and up on things because you're filling him in.

And, of course, you can always go back to your questions about him, because that is very likely his favorite subject.

Step 4: Acting the Part

What you say is only a portion of what attracts people to you. The other part is all the nonverbal actions and mannerisms that speak volumes. If you are going to be successful in dating or in any given endeavor, then you've got to get into a state that exudes confidence. This includes your internal dialogue (your thoughts or things you tell yourself), clothes, body language, eye contact, breathing and where you stand in relation to the other person or people. We've already discussed how to keep a healthy and constructive internal dialogue in Chapter 3. Now let's discuss the other aspects of your nonverbal presentation. Beginning with:

1 **Your style**—Men fall in love with their eyes, so looking your best is a must. That said, don't wear or do anything that isn't you. For instance, if you are wearing a dress that you can't breathe in just because it's slit-down-to-there sexy, I don't care how much it makes you look like Jessica Rabbit, your discomfort will show in the way you carry yourself. If your sweater is making you itch like a dog in dire need of a flea collar or your stiletto heels are making you as unsteady on your feet as a toddler, you won't be able to focus on the flirting at hand and may very well lose out to a girl who's relaxed and having herself a great old time in a shirt from Target and running shoes!

2 **The way you move**—About 90 percent of every opinion people form about you comes through their eyes first. So no matter how confidently you're chatting away, if your body language says you're insecure that's how you'll be perceived. When you are in conversation, avoid nervous habits like twirling your hair, shifting your weight back and forth or fidgeting. Instead of standing too close or staring too intently, stand at a comfortable distance. Too close feels as though you're invading his space. Too far makes you seem standoffish and unsure. You're going to laugh at my next suggestion, but practice your stance. Do it in front of the mirror. Do it in front of friends. Nail it and it'll make a difference.

If you ever watched that reality show, *The Bachelor,* where one guy dates something like twenty girls and eliminates a few each week, you've already seen some extreme examples of the effect of body language. Every week, there would be an elimination ceremony, during which the girls would stand side by side while the bachelor stood in front of them with a bunch of roses. The girls who received roses got to stay and the others didn't. As these women waited for him to call their names, their body language was loud and clear. You could easily tell which girls were desperate to make it to the next round and would be devastated if they didn't get a rose and which ones had enough confidence to know that they weren't going to die if they never saw this guy again. And you know what? It was usually the desperate girls who were sent packing and the confident ones who made it until the end. So make sure your body language is in line with the image you want to present—cool, calm, collected.

3 **Your placement**—Your positioning in any given room, whether a friend's living room or a club, says a lot about your availability. You don't necessarily want the gunfighter's chair—back to the wall and table in front of you—where the poor guy will have to suffer your *Dirty Harry,* "go ahead, make my day" stare from at least thirty paces

across the room. Here are some other positions that clearly scream: “Go away!”

- Huddled in a corner
- Standing with your back toward the crowd
- Sitting at a booth, safely out of eyeshot
- Sitting on a couch at a party where everyone else is standing
- Arms folded across your chest, eyes looking at the ground

And here are the positions that are likely to get you in someone’s crosshairs in no time:

- Standing at the center of interaction, in a heavily trafficked area
- Sitting at the bar
- Facing the crowd, looking around for opportunities

Dating Don'ts

A recent survey by the dating service *It's Just Lunch* reveals men's and women's pet peeves about dating. Almost 1,400 male and female singles were surveyed. Here's what they said.

- 46 percent say their biggest pet peeve is when their date answers a cell phone during a meal.
- 41 percent say their biggest pet peeve is their date being rude to the waitstaff of a restaurant.
- 26 percent of men and 37 percent of women can't stand when their date talks too much and only about himself or herself.
- 30 percent of men and women agree that talking about your ex on the first date is the quickest way not to get a second one.
- 45 percent of single men dislike it when their date talks about her weight or newest diet, and 56

percent of women say they hate it when their date is more interested in the waitress than them and shows it.

- 71 percent of men would accept a second date with a woman even if she displayed one of his pet peeves. However, only 42 percent of women feel the same way.

- Making rounds and mingling to get the most exposure
- Good posture, body relaxed, arms loosely by your side and shoulders down.

Of course, you shouldn't constantly be thinking about your posture, or you will come off as self-conscious. A good trick for forgetting about yourself and acting natural is to focus on your environment. Look at the people around you. Get immersed in the conversations you're having. Have fun!

4) **Your ability to connect**—Speaking of getting immersed in conversation, there

is no better way to stay focused on and engaged in a dialogue than making eye contact with the other person. There is something very disarming about a woman who will look you in the eye, hold a handshake a little longer, touch your arm to underscore a point she's making, or use your name midway through the conversation. This is the extra connection that will make the person you're speaking to feel good about himself, the experience and, most important, you.

One of the principles that I used to teach in witness training was that if you wanted to be effective in persuading other people, you needed to pay attention to the impact your demeanor was having on them. Specifically, I taught what I learned through our research: that we tend to believe those we like and that we tend to like those who we perceive as liking us. We all like to feel acceptance. If witnesses were angry or withdrawn because they did not want to be in court, the jury often perceived that as rejection and reacted very poorly to the witnesses who seemed to have a wall up, and acted cold and distant. The jurors took it personally. They didn't feel liked, so they tended to not like the witness, which meant they tended to not accept what the witness was saying. Exactly the same thing is true with you. If the man you're talking to feels accepted and liked by you, he is much more apt to like you in return. I always taught people to be warm toward the jury, to make eye contact with the jurors. Pick out one or two people like you and make sure to look at them. So if a witness was forty years old, was a female and had three kids at home, she should look at jurors number three and number seven because they're in the same situation. You don't pander to them; you just connect with them. This is genuine and real, not coming from a place of manipulation. The same goes for the dating world.

Mirroring is another key skill that could put you at the top of your social arena. If you pay attention to the nonverbal communication of the person you are speaking to, then approximate that person's posture and tone and mirror it back to him, you will create an immediate bond. If he is standoffish, let him know by your standoffishness. There will be an unconscious connection. When people are mirrored, they feel understood. Listen to how a guy describes things, and mirror him verbally and physically. Talk in his terms, his language.

Your voice and speech count, too. When people are nervous they often speak in a hushed, monotone voice, so make sure to speak clearly and do not be afraid to express enthusiasm, disappointment, joy or any appropriate emotion in your tone. Again, this will make the person you're speaking to feel that he's really getting to know the real you. If you are generous with your feelings, you will make whomever you're speaking with feel that he knows you too well to stand on formality. And there is your connection right there—so don't act so surprised when he slips you his business card or, even more likely, asks for your number and actually calls.

Step 5: Starting the Connection

Thanks to your well-thought-out and carefully executed plan of attack, you've met a guy or two who may have potential. You've been out a few times and it's pretty clear that he's interested, too. This is where you've got to employ a strategy and have a good game plan. Be careful, be deliberate and be purposeful in your actions so that you elicit more of the reactions you want and less of the ones you don't.

First let's talk about communication. You and your female friends probably check in regularly with each other, maybe once, maybe twice or maybe three times a day (though I've got no clue how you have so much to talk about). But guys aren't like that. For example, one time I was talking to a buddy who had just got engaged and asked him if he thought his friends and family back east would be surprised and he said, "The ones who didn't know I was dating will be." That may be a bit extreme but not completely shocking. Remember, communication is not usually a guy's strong suit, and overload can cause him to shut down. It's even more of a challenge today when there are so many ways to reach out and touch someone. Let's start with the phone.

1 **Phone etiquette**—Giving him a ring at the office or on his cell too many times a day or at inappropriate times "just to say hi" or "just to check in" won't remind him how much he misses you. It will put you on par with telemarketers and might make him wonder if dating you is going to be another full-time job. Calling to check in may push a guy's panic button, and ensure that every time his phone rings he checks his caller I.D.; if it's your number, you're going straight to voice mail and then delete.

If he begins to feel that you're invading his space or that you're checking up on him, not only will you look desperate and needy, but he will start trying to claw his way out of this relationship. In the first month, you should allow him to initiate contact at least half the time. This way, not only do you not smother him and make him feel you're putting on the pressure, but you get a clue as to his level of interest (or lack thereof). **Treat your urge to dial like a food craving and do something else for thirty minutes to see if it passes.** Call a friend, go for a run (but not over to his place!) or better yet, do your nails so it's difficult to dial him up. This method will also buy you enough time to realize that you've already called him four times, and it's not even lunch.

As for cell phones, take note of how he uses his. Does everyone from his dentist to his dad call him on it or does it rarely ring? Is it for emergencies only? The worst thing is to call him at an inappropriate time, like while he's in the middle of an important client meeting or in church. This will embarrass him and he won't feel too good about you. If you do call and sense he wants to hang up, you need an exit strategy. Here's a good one: Be the one who initiates the good-byes. If you sense that you caught him at a bad time, say, "Oh, I've got to run. Let's talk when we both have more time."

2 **E-mail and text savvy**—E-mail and text messaging make it easy to keep that connection alive without looking too eager. You can drop him a line on his computer or his phone once in a while, but don't forward him jokes, e-mail him five times a day or fill his phone with cutesy texts. To you, it may seem sweet and playful to send a message that says, "I can't go five minutes without thinking about you!" To him, it means he'd better check the bushes outside his place every night to make sure you're not lurking in them. He will log off quickly, and soon your e-mails and messages will be blocked faster than a rained-out road. When he gives you a buzz or zaps you an e-mail, don't respond instantly. Let him get himself worked up wondering what you're so busy doing. Believe me, if you let him sweat it out a little bit, he'll be that much happier when you finally return his call.

You're moving along and are actually dating this guy. Here's where you've got to be willing to play some poker. Some people may call this playing "hard to get," but that's not really it. You don't want to run him down like a cheetah on a deer. You want to make him come to you, like a deer comes to the feeder.

After the early phases of the interaction have passed and you're dating, you've still got to remain mysterious. I don't care how passionately he proclaims his love for you, or how much you're dying to show him that you feel the same way, you need to stay on your guard and not overcommit in the beginning. That means not seeming too eager. It means not always saying you're free when he calls you up (even if laundry's the only thing on your agenda). And it definitely means not saying "yes" to plans with him if he calls you at 5:00 P.M. on Saturday to go out that night. If you are always available, going out with him, calling him up, sending e-mails, you're ruining the mystery and taking all the fun out of the getting-to-know-you

First Date: Dos and Don'ts

You never get a second chance to make a first impression. Make sure you don't blow it. Follow these rules:

Do:

1. *DO make sure that you're listening as well as speaking. Ask him questions and pay attention to his answers. Then wait for him to ask you something before launching into your stories.*
2. *DO smile when you greet him and laugh at his jokes. This will make him feel that you're both having a great time.*
3. *DO maintain good eye contact. Looking him in the eye will heighten the attraction.*
4. *DO use your filler questions whenever there is a lull in the conversation. This will avoid awkward silences and make him think you're really interested in what he has to say.*

5. DO be safe. Keep your date in a public place until you've gotten to know him a little better.

Don't:

1. DON'T get drunk. You'll lose perspective and start making bad judgments.
2. DON'T neglect your grooming and predate prep work. Just because you don't think he's the man of your dreams right away doesn't mean he can't sweep you off your feet. And when he does, the last thing you want to think is, "Darn, I wish I had worn something a little nicer."
3. DON'T reveal too much personal information. Keep the conversation positive and light.
4. DON'T go on and on about your ex. He'll think you're still not over him.
5. DON'T be late. You don't want to start off by annoying your date.

process. You're making things so easy for him that he's not intrigued. It may sound obnoxious, but what's the point of committing to you if he's already got you? We all want what we can't have. You need to remain that carrot on a stick—elusive and always just barely out of reach. Every woman fears being taken for granted. What I'm giving you is a way to prevent that.

Guys value things they have to work hard for. It's the reason they're so loyal to their fraternity because they go through hell to get into it. They do shots until they throw up, run naked through the campus when it's thirty-one below and eat things they wouldn't give to a pig. After all that, they convince themselves it must be a great place to join or why else would they have put up with all that? Dating is the same way. A guy doesn't value a woman if he doesn't have anything invested in her. That is why guys suddenly want a woman that they didn't even notice as soon as someone else shows interest in her.

Prolonging the anticipation, and maintaining a little mystery about yourself, tantalizes him. There always has to be a tease. If you read the last chapter of a novel before you even start the book, you don't read the book with urgency. You want to be a page-turner; someone who holds things in reserve so he has something to look forward to. He'll appreciate you even more, since he's put in overtime hunting you down. I knew a guy who met a woman on jury duty. They spent several hours talking while they waited to be called. He wasn't really all that interested, but he still decided to ask her out and then go from there. Then she pulled out her Blackberry and they tried to schedule a date. Her calendar was so packed she couldn't see him for two weeks. All of sudden this girl he was on the fence about was the girl he was dying to go out with. Make your guy play the waiting game. If he wants to hook up this weekend, tell him you can't until next weekend—and don't offer an explanation. If he asks what you're doing, respond with a vague answer like, "It's just not a good night" or "I've got plans with a, um, a friend." If you're always available, you'll bore him. But if he's vying for your time (and wondering if you're spending some of it with another guy), he gets a little competitive.

This theory applies to sex as well. If you hop in bed up front, there is no mystery, no intrigue. That's different for each person and each couple, but better to keep him guessing about when, where and what it will be like than showing him everything you've got too soon. Waiting will only make him want you more. Men expect women to fall in love fast, so never let him think you're a goner—even if you are. Keep the "L" word out of your vocabulary for a while. Otherwise he'll feel too pressured to either say it too or talk about the future with you, and he'll probably pull back. Even if he has strong feelings for you, the fact that you're so out in the open about everything can make him feel that it's all going too fast, and he'll want off the ride. At this point, skip the "are we boyfriend-girlfriend?" conversations. Guys are always bracing for that moment when your nights of marathon sex are preempted with marathon talks "about us." Just hold off. Enjoy the game and don't show all your cards at once.

8

Fishing with a "Net"

The Internet is the most important single development in the history of human communication since the invention of call waiting.

DAVE BARRY

Have you ever sat around discouraged about your love life and thought, "I couldn't catch a date with a net!"? Well, that seems to be an old saying that we are going to have to throw out with yesterday's newspaper. Thanks to hundreds of dating websites, "You've got mail" can now be "You've got male" or, sometimes, "You've got junk male." Join one and each day you just might find responses from several men in your inbox. Dating pre-Internet was like fishing with one line in a small pond. Add the web to your dating arsenal and you're casting your net into an endless ocean. (I'm glad these matchmaking sites weren't around before I met Robin. With such a huge network out there and all the choice she'd have, I probably wouldn't have stood a chance!) By now you've probably got at least one friend or friend of a friend who's tried to find love with the click of a mouse. And your friend isn't alone. Online dating experts tell me that every month 61 million people log on and each year they shell out $473 million on Internet dating. Now it's as common a way to meet someone as a blind date or the bar scene, and you can connect with people of all ages, religions, professions and backgrounds from all over the globe. Online dating can be a great tool for broadening your options as long as you are smart, are cautious and take some very important safety steps, which I'll talk about in detail later in the chapter. If you do that, then your computer can be a highly efficient way to screen some potential dates. It just might save you a long evening with some guy who is about as much fun as a root canal. For the most part people on online dating sites are regular people just like you. They might work in the same office building two floors below you, but you never meet because you arrive at work fifteen minutes earlier than they do.

You may think online connections aren't for you, and that's okay. But sometimes you have to do something that's a little different, a little outside your comfort zone, to get what you want. Maybe online dating is intriguing to you, but you think there is a stigma attached, such as the idea that only "desperate" people do it. That may have been true even a few years ago, but we are a computerized society and it is now regarded by many as the cutting-edge way to "let your fingers do the walking." Some people are judgmental about online dating and pooh-pooh it as an alternative because it's not traditional and it seems like advertising for a date. But are more traditional places to meet men, like bars and clubs, anything more than meat markets? They're often poorly lit, smoke-filled and so loud that your conversation consists of yelling three-word answers. And let's face it, some of those old boys, shall we say, just "don't take much to light!" In other words, when you get them into the daylight they don't look quite so good! You may not come away from that type of meeting with information that's at all superior to what you get from an exchange on an online dating site.

The truth is that there are advantages to each method. A bonus for the live date is that you get to look him in the eye and get the scoop on him from interacting person-to-person. A bonus for online dating is that you see his photo and profile and get to evaluate him before actually meeting him. You can also have a rational and reasonable exchange so if you choose to actually meet, you'll have more information about him than you would have about a stranger you meet in a club. How reliable is the information you get online? That's questionable, and you must take great precautions to protect yourself against being misled.

❤♡

Before you ever have a face-to-face meeting with an online individual, I highly recommend that you do verify what you're being told by using your computer or, if possible, with a third party. But you should do that no matter where you meet someone.

You should do this if you meet him at a party, your office or your church (yes, church!) You should do this if you get set up—even if a close friend or relative did the matchmaking. I think it's important that you not take anything at face value, either. The world is full of bad actors, and you've got to be responsible for your own safety and security.

Who's Online?

A recent survey found that:

- 98 percent of single men are looking for a long-term relationship.
- 94 percent of single men said they're ready to balance both a serious relationship and a career.
- 87 percent think it's sexy to date a woman who earns more than they do.
- 79 percent of single men have contributed to a charity in the past year; one in three currently volunteers in his community.
- 75 percent of single men said their ideal woman would be their best friend; kindness was rated the most important attribute in a potential partner.
- 58 percent of single men have been cheated on.
- 57 percent of single men say they believe in love at first sight.

- 56 percent say a girl who sleeps with them on the first date is great, but not the marrying kind.

Getting Started

I talked to industry leaders and watchdog groups to get information on the ins and outs of this relatively new mode of dating as well as the pros and cons. Here's what they told me. Before you get started, make sure you've got some free time to read and respond to all the e-mails you're going to get right after you post your profile. They say that's when you're the new girl in town and get a lot of attention (especially in small cities where there aren't many new profiles posted each day). Be sure to verify information of a potential match, whether you find him online or on the town. You will also want to create a different e-mail address for the dating world that's separate from your real-life one. Many sites make this easy by giving you a free e-mail account. Not only is this good for managing all the guys who may be contacting you, but once you've received your very own e-male, you won't have to worry about the lingering trail of suitors clogging your personal mailbox. Even if you don't decide to set up a new account, definitely don't date online at the office, since some companies monitor employees' use of the computer. Experts advise these safety tips:

Cyber Safety

- ✔ Verify information on a potential match as thoroughly as possible.
- ✔ Always create a separate e-mail account for your online dating activity.
- ✔ Get a post office box, rather than using your home address, to register for the dating site. (Do this for all sites where an address is required.)
- ✔ List your cell phone number, not your home number, if the site requires one.

- ✔ Change your cell phone billing address so it goes to your P.O. box. That way, if some nut has access to a backward phone book (one with phone numbers in numerical order with addresses listed) he can't look up your address.
- ✔ When chatting or e-mailing, never give more than a first name, and keep it that way until the first date.
- ✔ Install a privacy checker on your computer. This lets you set privacy standards and be alerted when a dating site doesn't meet them. These checkers are often free and can be downloaded online.

With hundreds of sites out there and more and more launching all the time, you're bound to find at least one that works for you. There are sites for most ethnic groups and religious backgrounds and international sites (for those who like to earn frequent flier miles while they date). For example, there are sites for Christian and Jewish singles, for those over the age of thirty and for single professionals. Some have large databases you can search, and others promise your ideal partner because you fill out an extensive compatibility questionnaire. There are free sites and sites that cost upwards of $50 a month. Which is right for you? The only way to answer this question is to log on and poke around. Lots of sites give you a free trial period so you can check them out and acclimate yourself to their system and buffet of prospects. In fact, I know one woman who is now exclusively dating a man she met during her free trial period. (She got a bargain and a boyfriend in one!) Notice which ones have fill-in-the-blanks style profiles that ask all the crucial questions and which have free-flow profiles that may show lots of personality but also allow the writer to selectively omit important data. One caution: Experts say there are many Internet sex sites and mail-order-bride websites, both of which disguise themselves as online dating. It'll be pretty obvious to you when you visit one of them, but be careful.

Once you've joined a site, chances are it

will ask you to create a combination of six to ten letters and numbers, called a user I.D. or screen name. This is the first thing potential dates "see" of you. It's your first impression, so make it work for you. Try to say something about yourself here without being too complicated or confusing. You don't need a name that's too cute or clever, just one that's memorable or that says a little bit about you like "RunnerGirl" or "MarathonMaggie." But don't try to be excessively hip or witty or give your whole résumé in your I.D. Less is more. "Sandy143" is often better than "PhdFitCuteNYcallme." As much as you can attract or intrigue guys with your screen name, you can also send them running with "looking4mrRight," "UandMeForever" or "HereComesYourBride." You may be trying to be cute or funny, but most guys won't get the joke.

Industry insiders tell me that when looking for love on the Web, one key to attracting guys is your "profile," which is basically a statement about yourself. They say the most successful profiles reflect who you are, present you in your best light and give would-be responders a glimpse of what it'll take to win your heart. Though you want to give enough information to be intriguing, you don't want to give every single detail about yourself. Not only is that boring; it leaves nothing left for a future date to find out. Write the way you talk, and be very specific, sincere and honest. And most of all, show your personality. Go back to Chapter 5 to choose the qualities that really show the Character of You. Stay away from generic adjectives—"fun," "happy," "smart," "romantic"—since there are about 1,000 fun, happy, smart, romantic girls signed up at the same site.

Show, don't tell, experts say. Include stories about yourself that illustrate those traits. For instance, rather than saying that you are "successful," say that you've "raced up the corporate ladder with three promotions in less than two years" or that you really "get a charge out of closing a large deal." Instead of describing yourself as "funny," tell the story that had your friends laughing until their stomachs ached. If you're "athletic" talk about the 5K or marathon you just ran. An anecdote or two paints a clearer picture of you than a laundry list of adjectives does.

If you think you're thirty pounds over the average woman be proud that you are "more woman to love" or "voluptuous." If you are a single mother—of four—put "supermom" high on your list of accomplishments. Some man will respond to that. Honesty is important, too. Don't talk about your long legs if you stand only five feet tall. Eventually you're going to have to post a photo and may meet him in person and the cat will be out of the bag. Why waste your time and his?

Don't omit important information even if you think it will limit the number of men who contact you. One online dating expert I spoke to told me about a guy who met a woman online. She seemed to be his match. They had great e-mail conversations for a week or so, and he couldn't wait to meet her in person. Then she revealed that she had two young children. She told him that she didn't include this in her profile because she didn't want to scare men. Well, that's a big one and something people should know up front. This guy wasn't ready for an instant family and didn't want to suddenly play dad to two kids. In fact, he wasn't sure he ever wanted kids of his own.

When describing what you want in a man, be specific but don't scare him off or send the wrong message. You may long for a tall, handsome, rich Mr. Right, but don't include a superficial wish list about wealth or looks. Instead of rich, ask for "ambitious." Instead of "hot body," mention your desire for someone who likes to work-out. You may be very eager to get married, but I wouldn't say that you're "looking for someone to walk down the aisle with." Peruse the Character of Him that you created in Chapter 2 and mention some of those important traits.

Online dating insiders say writing a profile is worth your time, because it will ultimately help you find the right type of person and enable the right person to find you. You may feel overwhelmed by having to pen your profile (especially if the last time you wrote anything was in high school), but give it a shot. And if you think it's better to have your friend the English major do it for you, think again. When you write something, it's in your voice, and that will help you make a connection with someone better than perfectly polished prose that doesn't sound like you. (You can always ask your pal to proofread it.)

Questions to Ask

Experts suggest asking yourself these questions before you write your profile.

1. *What's special, unique, distinctive, or impressive about you or your life story?*
2. *What details of your life, personal or family challenges, history, people or events have shaped you or influenced your life goals?*
3. *What have you learned about past relationships, in terms of yourself?*
4. *What are your relationship goals?*
5. *Have you had to overcome any unusual obstacles or hardships (for example, economic, familial or physical) in your life?*
6. *What personal characteristics (for example, integrity, compassion, persistence) do you possess, and how can you demonstrate that you have these characteristics?*

7. *Why might you be a stronger candidate than other women?*
8. *What is the single most compelling reason you can give a guy to be interested in you?*

Overcoming Photo-Posting Phobia

Probably the most difficult part about taking the plunge into the sea of online dating is that you've got to post a photo to get a lot of hits, according to experts. They say a faceless profile just doesn't get as many. At least you can find comfort in the fact that the guys online went through the same trauma you are experiencing about posting a photo. Unless he's Orlando Bloom, a man doesn't like to pose for the cameras any more than he likes shopping. Another reason some people are photo-phobic is the fear of being spotted by someone they know. Usually that fear is much worse than the embarrassment you'll feel if it actually happens. Think of it this way: If someone you know spots you on a site, it means he or she was dating online as well.

Recently, my researchers surfed a few dating sites and looked for various categories of women. It's amazing how many women use blurry, badly lit pictures to introduce themselves. It's even more shocking to see that many make the scenery or their dogs the main attraction. Guys aren't going to e-mail you just because they like your pet or the sunset behind you. Clearly show him the real you so you don't waste his time or yours. Here are a few clear ground rules for posting photos, as told to me by industry insiders. Some may seem like common sense, but my researchers found every "don't" you could imagine (and some you couldn't).

Dos	*Don'ts*
Do include a photo of your head and shoulders that is in focus and well lit.	Don't use just an extreme close-up.
Do use the most recent photo you have.	Don't use any photo more than six months old or more than five pounds thinner.
Do smile. (You'd do it to get approached in a club, wouldn't you?)	Don't frown. Angry, sad or pensive expressions aren't attractive.
Do use a photo with good lighting and one that is not over- or underexposed.	Don't use a blurry, grainy shot. It looks as if you're hiding something.
Do wear the style of clothing you always wear.	Don't dress like someone you're not. Clothes send a message. The wrong ones can

say the wrong thing about you.

- Do show a bit of your body. You're not looking for any man; you're looking for the one who's interested in who you really are.
- Don't hide behind other people or a couch or shopping bags. Show the real you.

- Do use color photos.
- Don't use black-and-white photos. They don't stand out on a page with other women's color shots.

- Do have someone else take the photo (or at least use a self-timer).
- Don't take a picture of yourself in the mirror!

How to Read His Profile

Now that you've mastered your profile, it's time to master his. My researchers tell me most sites will let you narrow your search on the basis of age, height, zip code, and so on. Once you pull up a page full of smiling targets you may have to do some work to decide who to contact. Some sites allow you to browse without any of the guys knowing that you've perused their profiles (until you contact them). But other sites function like a singles bar; he'll see you checking him out (and may decide to contact you first).

When you read a profile, think about two things. First, why does he feel the need to highlight a certain feature? Second, what has he omitted? You can try to read his profile the way you'd read a real estate ad: "Quaint home that needs a little TLC" is probably a very small dump. "Luxury living at an affordable price" means it's in a bad neighborhood. Note any glaring omissions. If he doesn't mention height, maybe he feels a little sensitive about being short. If he doesn't mention his job, then maybe he doesn't have one. Still, there's always a chance that his descriptions are totally accurate and his omissions mean nothing, so don't be too harsh. You can always e-mail him and ask him about these things.

After you've found someone who piques your interest, it's time to send an e-mail. When you do, be specific about something you saw in his profile. This shows that you actually read it and aren't just sending a mass e-mail to every guy on the site. If you have something in common, mention that. And end the e-mail by giving him something to respond to. A good way to do that is to ask a question like, "You said you're from Chicago. I am, too. Where did you grow up?" or "You said you loved that book. Have you ever read this one by the same author?" This is also a great opportunity to ask him some specific questions about himself. Make these both fun, like "If money were no object, what would you do and where would you live?" and serious, like, "Are you close with your family?" The more information you get, the more easily you can figure out if this e-male is worth meeting in person.

Predate Prep

As I mentioned earlier, it is a really good idea to do as much as you can to verify the information you have been given before you go face-to-face with your online date. You should actually do this before meeting anyone—man or woman—whether you met online, at a Knicks' game, at the park or through a friend. You owe yourself that information.

Having lots of information about your online prospect can help you weed out the creeps from the keepers.

Knowing if your guy is hiding something can prevent a future disappointment and may save your neck.

Also, do a Google search of his name, which will tell you if any information about him has appeared in the media or on a website. Who knows what will turn up? Maybe nothing, maybe just some interesting info or maybe some scary stuff you're glad you know before canceling on him. But there are a few things to consider. The information you find could be wrong or on the wrong guy (who happens to have the same name). The less information you insert when doing a search, the more likely you are to get a false hit. You could also discover information that was accurate at one time but that he has since remedied. Perhaps he went bankrupt twelve years ago when he had to quit his job to take care of his ailing parents. Snippets of information just don't tell you the whole story, and good news is often harder to find than the bad.

Give him only your first name before the date. When it comes to the logistics of the meeting, choose a public place you're familiar with—like a local mall, coffee shop, bookstore and so on—not his place or yours, and bring a friend. If you can't find a friend to come with you, don't go. Do not meet alone and do not meet in a private place. Make sure you tell someone you trust all the details of when and where you're meeting this guy and give her his photo and screen name. Make a plan to check in with her at a certain time. I'm not trying to make you paranoid, but I do want you to be safe. Naturally, if you feel any uncertainty when you see him or get a weird vibe that something's wrong, don't dismiss it. Follow your gut and make your exit, pronto.

Meet during the day, which may be safer since it's light out. And here's a biggie: No matter how much you're attracted to him on date number one, don't get into his car or accompany him to any private place. Make the date short, too. Tell him ahead of time that you have only fifteen minutes. Trust me, if he's not your man, fifteen minutes will drone on like an hour. If he's a fabulous catch he'll understand and respect your desire to protect yourself. With each successive date you can begin to let down your guard bit by bit as you would in the real world. But ease into the relationship. Meet his friends, his family and his coworkers. The truth is that you're vulnerable with anybody, but taking precautions can help keep you safe.

The Real-Life Meeting

Set realistic expectations for this date. First of all, he may not look exactly like the guy on your computer screen. Unlike dating in the real world, online dating is anonymous until you decide to reveal yourself. Hiding behind a computer makes it easy for anyone to tell a few white lies. Some guys (and women, too) shave a few years off their age, post photos of themselves ten years earlier or twenty pounds ago or Photoshop hair onto their balding heads.

For some people their online connection spills over into real life and you click. One of my producers said her e-mails and phone conversations with her current boyfriend made them feel so connected that their first date was like their tenth. There was no getting-to-know-each-other awkwardness because they'd already done that online. Then again, no matter how well you two match "on paper" or how connected your e-mails, IMs or phone conversations were, no computer can perfectly match for chemistry, that mix of sights, smells and sounds that happen when you're with someone in the flesh. So don't be too surprised or upset if fireworks don't go off the second you see him. This doesn't mean that he's not for you. During e-mail relationships there's a degree of emotional intimacy that happens when you feel protected by the anonymous world of the Internet. If he's been very revealing, he may just feel very exposed when the two of you are face-to-face and be a little nervous (the same goes for you). Give him time to warm up. On the flip side, you may have amazing spark with him online and then meet him for coffee and wonder, "What was I thinking?" He may have been witty and charming in the cyberworld, but in the real world he is a total dud. Sure, he runs his own business. He just failed to mention online that his business is selling old comic books from his parents' basement—where he lives.

Then again, maybe your date won't seem interested in you. No one likes rejection, but it happens. So don't go into the face-to-face meeting thinking that this is going to be the love of your life. If he's uninterested, it's no big deal and it's good to know this early on before getting involved. If you're uninterested, you've wasted only an hour and the cost of a cup of coffee. Sure, you can feel disappointed, but don't let it get in the way of your dating. Focus on what you can do, which is move on to the next e-male. Don't let a bad experience keep you from living your life to the fullest. You can go through life being distrusting or loving and laughing.

The bottom line is that as long as you act with caution, the Internet can be an efficient, productive and exciting target-rich environment. And you get to do it all from the comfort of your own home, wearing fuzzy slippers and sweatpants. What could be better than that?

9

Infrared Dating

You can tell a lot about a fellow's character by his way of eating jellybeans.

RONALD REAGAN

Let's just cut to the chase. When you're sitting there with your date discussing the latest contestant to be voted off the reality TV show of the moment, you're not really interested in his thoughts on the world of television. What you really want to know is "Do I like him a little or a lot and will this guy marry me if that is what I want, how does he feel about having children and is he going to treat me well?" Correct? Sure, you can talk about other stuff, figure out what interests and pursuits you may have in common, but I don't care how fun, nice, good-looking or compatible that guy is, if he says, "I ain't ever getting married. Not now or ten years from now," you're probably not going to invest a whole lot of time, effort and energy into creating a romantic relationship with him.

So how do you find out if a guy you are interested in is husband material without coming right out and saying, "Enough chitchat, buddy boy. I don't care what your sign is or how you feel about all this rain we've been having! Where do you stand on commitment?" That's where I come in. I'm going to tell you the cues, questions and observations that will lead you to what you want to know and tell you how to reliably get that information as best you can and as soon as you can. That is what this chapter is about—empowering you with information-gathering tactics that will start real, substantive conversations and set up key situations for you to observe in order to get the real scoop on where you are and could be headed.

I have developed a series of questions

and guideposts that you can, with considerable reliability, use to predict where these guys will come down on the issues that really matter to you—marriage, family, respect and values. The difference between these questions and more superficial ones like, "What's your favorite Web site?" "What kind of music do you like?" and "What kind of car do you drive?" is that the questions in this chapter will accomplish two crucial tasks in short order. First, they will provide you with the kind of answers and behavioral observations you can analyze to learn whether the guy sitting across from you has long-term relationship potential or if you're going down a dead-end street. And second, they will lead to discussions and observations that will help you figure out if he's got major flaws, if he'll treat you well and if he'll be a good father—because the last thing you want is a guy who says, "I want to marry you, give you babies and treat you like a queen, but please don't mind my daily drinking binges, insane bouts of jealousy and irrational behavior!"

I know it's a tall order, but one of the things you learn pretty quickly in my profession is that you have to spend as much time listening for what isn't being said as you spend listening to what is. You have to spend time observing what people do or don't do to determine if their behavior is congruent with what they say or if they play a different game from the one they talk.

I spent fifteen years as a trial consultant, and part of my duties involved jury selection. I had to evaluate where people stood on critical issues on the basis of limited information. It was limited because the judge would allow us to question the jurors and observe only their behavior very briefly before we made choices. Like you, I obviously could not ask what I really wanted to know, which was, "If I pick you for the jury will you vote for our side?" I had to cloak the questions and ask about things that may have seemed irrelevant but would lead me directly to what I wanted to know—all the while leaving the juror and the opposing attorneys none the wiser about what I had learned. I had to observe how the jurors behaved with each other and in reaction to our attorneys. Did they respond differently to male versus female lawyers? Did age make a difference? Did race make a difference? Did we like their answers to questions? Did we like their background? How did a male juror relate to female jurors? Was he kind or was he condescending? Was he a leader or a follower? Was he smart or not? Was he well-groomed or slovenly? For example, by doing pretrial research, the results of which the other side did not have, we could correlate questions we did ask with questions we weren't allowed to ask. We could then predict with a decent degree of reliability that people who answered yes to question 2 would also answer yes to ten other questions we weren't allowed to ask. Furthermore, by paying careful attention to the jurors' nonverbal communication as well as listening to what they actually said, I would get a clear and concise picture of the type of person I was dealing with. We knew because of pretrial preparation and research whether a business background was what we needed or not, whether affluence would be helpful or hurtful and so forth. We knew going in because we did our homework. With preplanning and some basic knowledge, finding the kind of person we were looking for was possible.

Tall order—but doable for me then and for you now. You don't have a trained staff of researchers (your mother doesn't count), but with some preplanning, between us we are going to come up with questions to use and observations that will tell you plenty and quickly.

After you've satisfied your curiosity and decided that this guy is on the up-and-up, you can make an informed decision as to how you feel about him, how much he fits the "Character of Him" that you developed in Chapter 2 and how much consideration you should give to the chemistry you're feeling whenever you lock eyes. Bottom line: You'll know whether you should put any more effort and energy into developing this relationship or whether it's time to start thinking of him in the past tense.

But before we get into talking about how you will find out exactly what you need to know, a few words of warning: The questions, by design, do not have "face validity," meaning that they may not seem to address what you really want to know. That's actually a good thing because you won't give away what it is you are inquiring about, and so you cut down on his telling you what you want to hear or stampeding for the door when he sees you coming. You don't want to look at the questions and warning signs that I'm about to give you and then dismiss them because they seem trivial. You have to listen for subtleties, make simple inferences and watch for patterns. While they are good predictors, these indications are far from 100 percent accurate, so you have to rely on all the info you have available—your observations of his tone, body language and behavior. And trust your own instincts. I know that women who are really focused on something have a great degree of discernment, so when you're paying attention, as I know you will be, listen to your own thoughts and beliefs.

Later, we will talk about how to ask these questions and gather the observational data in ways that do not make you seem to be cross-examining a hostile witness in a hotly contested trial or tracking some guy like a bounty hunter. In the meantime, let's take the five critical areas of interest one by one, point by point. Beginning with the biggie:

Will He Marry Me or Is He Commitment-Phobic?

Much as you may want to sit this boy down and ask him, "Just what exactly are your intentions, Mister?" you know full well that by doing this you'll only succeed in scaring him off. Instead, you'll have to pitch him some indirect, "softball" questions that will tell you a lot about his thoughts on marriage without causing panic. You can be as forthcoming as you choose at any point you choose, but if you want a solid sense of his values and you want it early on so you know whether or not you are wasting your time regarding long-term potential, inquire as to the following:

1 **His social life:** Getting him to talk about his friends and activities should be no problem. If he didn't think his social life was interesting, he wouldn't be doing it, right? Ask him, "What did you do last weekend?" "What do you usually do for fun?" Then pay close attention to what he says. What you're listening for is whether or not he makes excessive use of the word "we" (and I'm not referring to "we" as in you and him, but we as in him and his group of friends). If he hardly ever says "I" when discussing his goings-on, take it as an indication that your guy is very involved in a particular social scene or clique. Somebody who says, "I went to the game with Rob. Then I went fishing with a couple of buddies" is in an entirely different head space from a guy who says, "We went downtown and we couldn't find this club, so we ended up driving around all night. Then we

went back to Tony's and kicked it." That is a very immature, externally validated level of adjustment and probably indicates a low level of readiness for commitment or affiliation. You may have been in this mode in high school, or when you were in some other peer group or sorority mode. Again, this may seem trivial, but I can assure you that it is not.

If you are talking to somebody immersed in the "we" mode, you're not talking to somebody who is likely to make a commitment to you. Your timing is wrong, because you caught him at a time when he was measuring himself by the acceptance of his group. If men are in love with their group, they already have what you have to offer. It's that simple. They *already* are a part of something. They *already* have allegiances. They are *already* getting their emotional needs met by affiliation. They may have lost their identity to the group and would probably see you as a threat to their current social currency. Guys who think and talk this way are heavily peer-influenced. So if you're looking for a partner to devote his life to you and you only, your warning bells should be ringing loud and clear. A guy like this might be ready for a bachelor party, but not a wedding—at least not his own. Of course this is all a matter of degree. There's nothing wrong with having friends and at times being part of a "we." What I'm talking about here is someone who is stuck in that mode.

You can use the same information to figure out if someone is in fact ready for the next phase of his life to begin. You will find that some men who have been with the same old group for a long period of time have grown tired of it. The group's acceptance and validation have lost their magic. You can often tell when people are getting over their group, because they are no longer mesmerized by the "we" and the sense of belonging. Instead, they are starting to feel burned out, are sick of the scene and are lonely, hungry for intimacy rather than for collective group acceptance. They are wanting to settle down. This goes double for people whose group members are beginning to drop off into marriages and engagements. If a couple of a man's buddies are getting engaged, dates are being set and things are starting to change, you could predict that he is looking for his next place to land—and that may be with you. This guy is simply on a different point in the story arc of his social life. The "we" guy is in the early part of the arc and still climbing into the magic of belonging and acceptance in the group. The "I" guy is on the downslope of the arc, and the timing is right if you are right for each other. Remember what I said about landing guys who are One-Trick Ponies or who tend to compartmentalize—timing is everything.

2. **His past:** Say it with me: "The best predictor of his future behavior is relevant past behavior." A good relevant history is more powerful and predictive than any psychological test you could administer. His ultimate commitment

to you will be foretold by the pattern of the other commitments he's made in his life. That means you need to understand his commitment-relevant behavior in the past. Ask him:

- How long have you been at your job? In your career?
- Do you have a pet?
- How long have you lived in one place?
- How long have you had your car?
- How long have you known your closest friends?
- Have you ever had committed relationships before? For how long?
- How did those significant relationships end?
- Do you have a retirement account?

Remember, it's not the Spanish Inquisition. Don't go into interrogation mode by bombarding him with a list; just weave these things into your conversation and be very mindful of the answers. If this guy has bounced around from job to job, has switched careers three times in as many years, can't keep a plant alive much less a pet and moves at the drop of a hat, do I really need to tell you that he's probably not looking for a permanent copilot? Even if he is, he might not be the best bet for a long-term relationship. I'm not saying that people can't change, but this *is* relevant information, and it can either support or undermine the contention that someone is a good candidate for long-term commitment. Relevant past history tells a future-oriented story. You can justify, rationalize and explain away that history any way you want, but if you want to know what the boy's going to do next year, the best information you can gather is what he did last year.

I have been with my wife for thirty-five years and have been married to her for thirty years. We already know that fact about me, but if we didn't, what would an examination of my life on these dimensions predict about my willingness and ability to make a long-term commitment?

If I were single and people were meeting me and asking all these questions, they would discover the following information:

- How long has he been at his job? In his career?—I have had one career for thirty years and am currently in my third particular professional placement within the career. The first two were twelve to fifteen years in duration.
- Does he keep a pet?—I have always had pets, and I've kept the same cat for twenty-plus years. Currently, I have two dogs, one of which I have had for fourteen years.
- How long has he lived in one place?—I have always owned my homes for the last thirty-five years, and I average about five years per home.
- How long has he had his car?—I keep my cars for two or three years at a time.

- How long has he known his closest friends?—My closest friends and associates have been active in my life for thirty to thirty-five years and are currently still active relationships.
- Has he ever had committed relationships before, and for how long?—This one is obvious, since we know I've been married for thirty years.
- How did his other significant relationships end?—I dated Robin for several years before I married her, about thirty years ago. (Again, this is obvious—we already know the outcome.)
- Does he have a retirement account?—Absolutely.

You can see how all this information would help if someone wanted to predict exactly what kind of guy I am. Wouldn't that be a positive sign to you as well if you were trying to determine whether or not some man had the ability to commit and stay involved with you?

3 **His key people:** Ask him about the key people in his life, such as his parents, other respected adults in his life, siblings and closest friends, to see whether their experience with commitment has been good or bad. You can do this simply by asking, "Oh, what does she/he do? Is she/he married?" whenever he brings up a sibling or a friend. This is critically important information because those are the associations in his head. Those are the role models and influencers who are likely to mold his values and influence his views about committing to relationships. You learn what you live, so you need to understand what his experience with commitment has been. If his parents are or were happily married, that's very likely influenced his opinion of marriage. If they fought all the time and then divorced, that's a bad sign, because he's got the idea that marriage is no fun and doesn't last. Also, look to see if his close friends are

married or single. If the people he hangs with value marriage, chances are they're exerting at least subtle pressure on him to marry—which spells good news for your chances.

Will He Be a Loving and Nurturing Father?

If you are looking for not just someone to settle down with but someone to raise a family with, you need some additional information that is relevant to this consideration. Maybe you already have children and you want to know how the guy you are dating intends to parent them. Or perhaps you absolutely for a fact know that you do not want to shoulder the burden of parenting on your own while your husband thinks his entire role begins and ends with being a good sperm provider. Asking about these things too early in the relationship, however, will only get you an invitation to step out of his moving vehicle. Again, you can learn this important information across a few weeks instead of months of dating or—if the wrong answers and attitudes here would be a deal breaker—you can save yourself a lot of wasted time by asking and paying attention to the following:

1. **His family legacy:** You need to find out about his family experience and the type of relationships he had with his parents—especially his father. While he looks to his mother as the model for the mother of his own children, he considers his father's behavior as a standard of how the man of the house should behave.

   Talk to him about his family life. How often does he talk to his parents? How often does he make time to visit them? This will tell you how a high a priority he puts on family in general and whether or not he's got some of the makings of a family man. Also, make sure to observe what he does in the event of a family crisis. Does he put that relationship on project status or feel resentful and put-upon? Does he take time out of his work to go check on his father if the father has had a heart attack? If mom has major stress in her life, does he stop what he's doing to listen to her?

In short, how does he prioritize the events that are happening in his family and extended family?

To get the ball rolling, ask him, "What's your father like?" or, "What did you like to do with your father as a kid?" Then, pay careful attention to how he perceives his father's or stepfather's role as a parent. Take note of clues, hints or revelations of the following nature:

- Does he think that his father enjoyed the responsibility of being a parent? Did his father take that responsibility seriously?—This will tell you if he is looking forward to being a parent and whether or not he will view fatherhood as a positive, joyful experience.
- Was his father present and available, taking a sense of pride in the accomplishments of his children?—If so, you can predict that this guy will be available to his children. He'll go to the soccer games and the recitals.

He will be present when it's time to help with the homework or throw the ball in the backyard.

- Was his father aggressive? Domineering? Critical? Did he use corporal punishment?—The answer will tell you what style of discipline your guy is typically going to lean toward when it comes to his own children—or your children from a previous relationship.
- Did his father inspire fear? Respect? Both? Neither?—Guys want respect from their children. They want to be heard and effective. So how is he going to make that happen? Is he going to scare them into listening, or will he inspire them by becoming the hero, or will he bribe them with incentives?
- Overall, was his father a good model as a parent?—The way he judges his father's parenting style will have a lot to do with whether or not he's going to embrace his father as a role model. My father,

> for example, was an alcoholic. While I loved him, I didn't think he was a good model—and that is why I created a new model for myself.

These are critical cues to take into account, because the way he perceived his father's role will have a huge influence (negative or positive) on his desire and ability to be a parent.

If he doesn't want to follow in his dad's footsteps, then he is going to try establishing a new role that will be a sharp contrast to that of his father. But going against the flow takes a great deal of energy and concerted effort, so you have to be aware that things may be a bit more difficult for him than for someone who grew up in the kind of home he'd like to replicate.

Since parenting a family is a partnership, you should try to find out what he thinks of his parents' relationship. That will be the kind of partnership that he is most comfortable forming with you when it's time to start a family. So find out how his parents got along with one another. Did the father wear the pants? Did they work out their differences in front of him or behind closed doors, or did they never work out their differences at all? Again, understand that what feels most natural is what we grew up with. Any departure from that takes hard work. If he didn't grow up in a harmonious home, you need to watch what he says to find out if he seems willing and capable of creating one.

2 **His reactions:** Take him to a restaurant where there are a lot of families and kids making noise just to see how he reacts to the children. Or introduce him to some of your friends who have children of their own to see how he deals with them. Whether he's aloof and irritated or immersed in the

wonder and joy of childish innocence, take it as a real clue as to how he reacts to children in general.

Also, pay close attention to how he treats pets. If he has a dog or cat, is he a responsible pet owner? Watch for how he treats your pets as well. Does he refuse to walk your dog, or if he agrees, is he patient, or does he yank the dog and pull its leash?

3 **His general ideas on parenting:** Ask him the following questions or at least bring up stories or situations that generate answers to them or observations about them, to see what kind of parent he aspires to be:

- What responsibility should a parent take for the misbehavior of a child? (This question might be based on a current event.) Do you think parents should be held responsible if their kids are bullies?—Regardless of the position he takes, the conversation you initiate will tell you a lot about how important he thinks a parent's role is to the behavior and attitudes of a child.

- Were you ever bullied?—This is important because it will tell you how well he can relate to children's problems in general.
- How would you treat a child who hurt himself or herself or was ill?—Will he show tough love, or does he think total and absolute indulgence is the answer? The answer to this will tell you if he wants to spoil his kids rotten or whip them into shape before they hit puberty, or if he lies somewhere in between.

Obviously, there are no "right" or "wrong" answers here. What his answers will demonstrate, however, is the type of parenting style he admires and intends to follow. Again, I know you can't interrogate this poor guy; but with some finesse you will be amazed at how much you can learn.

A guy can be a great father to his children and still drive his wife up the wall on a daily basis. Before you sign on the dotted line, you need to figure out whether the man with whom you're considering merging lives is going to be good to you. Will he respect you? Will you be loved the way you want to be loved? Will you be listened to when you want to be heard? Will he be possessive, jealous and passionate or self-possessed, coolheaded and independent? Fortunately, you can use some of the observations you've already made to figure out what kind of husband the guy you are dating is likely to make. Start by analyzing:

1. **His family background:** Some of the material that you've already learned about his family can be applied here. One of the things you want to know is how his father treated his mother and how he treats her. This goes back to what I was saying earlier, because we learn the value of parental roles from our first models. If his father showed

respect to his mother and demanded that the children show her respect as well, you will find the son modeling that respectful behavior. If the father ignored the mother and her feelings and dreams, that's going to be typical of his son's behavior.

Again, pay attention to how the parents got along.

- How did they resolve conflict?—People have several ways of resolving conflict. They may try to battle it out as to who is right. Or they may squabble over minor things and avoid facing the critical underlying issues. Sometimes, they avoid all issues and conflicts, preferring to sweep them under the rug rather than risk a confrontation. At other times they find constructive ways to resolve their differences. Keep in mind that his parents will be his primary model for conflict resolution if you two get married.
- Did they communicate well or was there a lot of yelling in the

house?—This has to do with the kind of communication patterns he was exposed to. If most of his parents' conversations degenerated into shouting matches, he will express himself by shouting. This is a sign not of weakness so much as of lack of education. So if you know better, you may have some teaching to do.

- Did they support or undermine each other?—You want to know this because there are going to be times when you are going to be competitive with each other. You want to know if he can support you even if it costs him some of his own ego.
- Was his father proud of his mother, or critical and sarcastic?—Again, you will find that he will mirror his father's behavior toward his mother when interacting with you.

Believe me, if a guy comes from a home where people never raised their voices to one another, it will take nothing short of a four-alarm fire to get a rise out of him. On the other hand, if he comes from a home where yelling and screaming were the norm, buy some earplugs, because that's exactly what you can expect from him when push comes to shove. This is powerful, powerful information, so pay close attention to what you learn.

2 **Interpersonal behavior:** This is about how he behaves with you. Does he listen to you when you're talking? Does he say to you every other day, "You never told me that"? Do you get the sense that your thoughts and feelings are important to him? One single woman I know ended a relationship before it went any further when on her second date with a guy, he laughed at her for crying at a movie that he thought was dumb. She knew, right then, that not only was he unable to value her opinion, but he was also intolerant of her feelings.

Does he try to understand your frustrations and your celebrations? A lot of men don't understand why women celebrate the things they do, so you need to pay close attention to whether he can share in both your misery and your happiness. Will he take the time to be with you in times of difficulty as well as joy? If you're developing feelings for a guy, you may find it difficult to answer these questions honestly—but that's all the more reason for you to try your best to be as brutally honest as you can.

Also, pay attention to how easily he is distracted from you and your issues. If you repeat yourself constantly, and you both speak the same language, you may have a real problem. It may be hard for him to focus on you if he's got a lot of issues of his own, but if he tries, that's the critical part. Does he remember what you've told him—whether it's that your cat is sick, that your boss was rude to you, that your car got towed or that you came down with the flu? This is what tells you that you're important. If he calls up and says, "Oh, I forgot that you were in the hospital," that's a pretty clear sign that he's not thinking about you too much. If he stumbles now, he will stumble once you are married as well. On the other hand, if he remembers everything from your favorite ice-cream flavor to your dream vacation, you know he's had his mind on you.

Here are some additional questions to ask that can be real eye-openers:

- "How would you make a decision if you had a great job offer in Seattle and I had one in New York?"—His reaction will tell you a lot about how he sees your roles and whether or not he believes in an equal partnership.
- "If your mother did not agree with the way we were dealing with a family issue between ourselves, how would you handle that situation?"—Watch out for signs of divided loyalty. You want him to respect his mom, not fear her.
- Would he tell you little "white lies" just to make you feel better when

you were down, like "You look beautiful today" or "You look like you have lost weight"?—This will tell you what kind of a friend he will be to you when you're in need of some ego boosting.

3 **His relationships with women:** Look at the women in his life. His relationships with his female friends, coworkers and sisters can tell you a lot about how comfortable he is with women. If a man has one or more sisters, he has already had the experience of having to forge some working relationship with another female. That kind of experience is a plus (even if it wasn't particularly positive) because he's had to learn how to live in the same house as a girl and compete against her for his parents' attention.

How does he treat his mother now? Pay attention to how he speaks to her on the phone. Does he take her calls or does he screen them? How often do they speak? What tone of voice does he use when he's on the phone with her? Is it loving and affectionate, or cold and aloof? Is he even listening, or just letting her talk? As discussed in Chapter 6, this will tell you a lot about how he will treat you if you ever get married.

Does he have female friends? If he's never had a female friend, this may very well mean that he doesn't trust women. In that case, he may be afraid of you and may be likely to run away or get combative. If he has female coworkers, pay attention to how he speaks about them or gets along with them. Does he treat them as regular members of the team and socialize with them the way he does with the guys, or does he tend to look down on them and shy away from their company?

Does He Have Any Major Flaws?

Dating a con man is not something that happens only to other people. There are many fast talkers out there who know exactly what to say and exactly what you want to hear. Many women have been abandoned, tricked, bankrupted or just made completely miserable by these guys who seem to know exactly the right way to behave until they get what they want. These questions will help you figure out if you are dealing with a man of integrity or with a man who will become a nightmare in three months.

To see how well-balanced a guy is, take note of the following:

1 **His attitude toward his relationships:** Look out for any chips on his shoulders. If he feels that he got a raw deal from his family or past girlfriends, he is going to spend much of his life trying to even the score. He's going to be looking out for number one and feeling that he is entitled to act unfairly toward others. He may even be hungry for some reward that he feels the world owes him for his trouble, whether it's money, attention or recognition.

If he has a sense of entitlement,

that is a dead giveaway that this guy is trouble. You can sleuth this out by looking into his relationships with his friends and family members. Is he jealous of them? Does he borrow money from them? Does he seem to hold grudges? If you sense that he believes somebody owes him something, you may get the brunt of that unresolved frustration.

2 **Destructive habits:** If the guy drinks too much, chain-smokes or does drugs, there's your tip-off right there. He is not operating on a responsible mental plane. Normally, self-destructive people do not limit their damaging behavior to themselves. These are the very people who are most likely to behave irresponsibly toward you as well. Whether that means lying, cheating, stealing, putting you in harm's way or even losing their temper and getting violent, people who have shown a lack of control over their destructive impulses need to be avoided. You're not his therapist, and

the doorway to your house doesn't have twelve steps. Ask him:

- "What do you do to make yourself feel better when you are having a miserable day? Take drugs? Eat? Drink? Exercise? Spend money?"—This will show whether his stress-relieving habits are constructive or destructive. If he says he eats a pint of ice cream every night, for example, that may indicate a problem with self-control—and, I'm betting, cavities.
- "Will you tell the truth even if it makes you look bad or may hurt my feelings?"—This demonstrates integrity, or the need to stay true to one's values and ideals even when doing so isn't always easy.

3 **Moral issues:** In the course of any relationship, you are bound to run across a situation that allows you to observe how he deals with a moral

issue—one where he has a choice between doing what is right and doing what he wants. It could be something as seemingly minor as deciding whether to go to a family function or tell a white lie to get out of it, stopping to help someone in distress or pressing on to get where he's going on time, being rude to a store clerk or keeping his temper under control. Watch out for consistent patterns of behavior. For instance, does he always turn to distorting the truth in order to get his way? Does he always want to be right—even if that's at the cost of the relationship? And how does he react to frustration and not getting his way (whether with you or someone else)? Does he use aggressive and immature pressure tactics—like threatening to leave, using harsh words, begging or whining?

When you begin to see a questionable pattern of behavior, you can be sure that these problems will not go away. Left unchecked, character flaws tend to get worse, not better, so you need to be really clear about your zero-tolerance policy. In the beginning, the relationship may be the priority for the guy. As he gets comfortable, however, he will begin to choose his immature, destructive tendencies with increasing consistency. Again, without intervention, like therapy or some conscious and concentrated effort, this type of behavior typically does not go away. The older couple you see bickering in the food store has probably been having some version of that fight for fifty years.

How Well Does He Fit My Needs for the Character of Him?

If you recall, back in Chapter 2 we took great pains to figure out what you need and desire in a guy. You went through five major areas—personality, social skills, relational style, spiritual compatibility and appearance—to come up with an idea of the type of guy who will be your Mr. Almost Perfect, your Mr. 80 Percent.

We went through that exercise for a reason: to acknowledge that you have certain needs, wants and standards for your partner and that you're not going to go through the search process with a "beggars can't be choosers" attitude. So here we go again. Except that this time, you've actually got a real, flesh-and-blood guy sitting across the table from you. Whether or not you can see yourself settling down with him will depend on how he makes you feel and how well he fits in with the character of him. Overall, you want to feel that this guy is worthy of you, and that he has more of what you want in a partner and less of what you don't. To substantiate these feelings and beliefs, you must evaluate him on the basis of his merits. So remind yourself of those five categories, think of the 80 percent rule and begin to pay close attention to:

1. **Him without you:** Other people's observations can be a great resource. He's going to put his best foot forward when you're around, so you may want to watch him from a slight distance to keep your vision from being

distorted by emotions like love and caring.

To learn more about his personality and social skills, bring him to a party or a family function. Then step back and watch how he interacts with everyone. Since these people are close to you, you will immediately be able to tell whether or not they warm up to him as time progresses. Of course, once the party is over, you can collect everyone's feedback to see if they want to welcome him with open arms or bar him from the neighborhood.

2 **His résumé:** Most men will try to convince you that they're the smartest guy around. And while that may or may not be the case, you should look for some kind of qualifications or corroborating evidence.

- Look at his level of education. Is he a high school dropout?—If he quit high school before graduation, you want to find out why. Was it to join the military or for economic reasons? Was he motivated by other, possibly more pressing responsibilities, or by the avoidance of all responsibility? If he quit to do drugs and party, and worse yet, he doesn't regret it, you already know all you need to know about his sense of discipline and motivation, unless there is powerful and objective evidence of maturing.

- How successful is he in his work?—Having chosen his career, how is he doing in it? Is he happy or disgruntled? Does he feel limited? His feelings about his work and his plans for the future will tell you a lot about his potential.
- How successful is he in terms of the goals that he wants to obtain?—Whether he can set goals and achieve his goals will tell you a lot about his strength of character. If he's constantly having pipe dreams that he can never seem to execute, then he is always going to be looking for his ship to come in. He's always

> going to be looking to hit it big in some get-rich-quick scheme. But he doesn't really know how to be successful. He's not willing to put in the work needed for success. You want a guy who can be successful in any arena because that's the same effort he will apply to your relationship.

After your mid-twenties, you begin to develop a track record. Just like we talked about in the last chapter, do a Google search. It can yield a lot of information—some accurate, so not—but info nonetheless. If you see he's tried to start five businesses that have failed, you'll learn about his ability to follow through. There are a zillion excuses as to why we fail, and any of them could be legitimate, but what you have to look at is a pattern of failure.

You wouldn't believe how many times I've heard women say, "When I met him, he seemed so intelligent, he said all the right things. I cannot believe what a bum he turned out to be." Don't beat yourself up; it's normal to want to believe certain things. Show me a woman who doesn't want to believe that the guy who loves her is one of the greatest men alive, and I will show you a woman who couldn't spot the truth with a pair of field binoculars. Most people are fools for love, so you need to look at the evidence. Go to the real hard data.

3 **His values:** Get a deeper sense of how he is or isn't compatible with the Character of Him by checking out the following revealing information:

- If he could change something he did in his life, what would it be?—This is his opportunity to confess about past mistakes, and your opportunity to see how much he has learned from them.
- Is he religious or spiritual and does he follow a code of conduct?—This will tell you how grounded, serious, conscious and

purposeful he is about his everyday actions.

- Does he show respect for his friends and family by showing up on time, fulfilling promises and commitments, helping out?—If he goes out of his way for the people who have been in his life the longest, then he is likely to keep going out of his way for you through the years.

4. **His moods:** People can always look good when they feel good. But their real character comes out when they feel bad. When you're having the kind of day where even you know that you're hard to get along with, how does he respond to this? Does he have the patience and fortitude to hang in there with you and even make you laugh? How about when he's feeling low? How does he relate to you? Does he just shuffle off into his cave? Does he say ugly things to you so you won't talk to him? Or does he rise above his own moodiness and at

least put the effort out to show that you're important to him?

Also, pay special attention to what happens when you're in conflict and you're both in a bad mood. How do you argue, and how do you resolve the argument? This is the point at which relationships get either deeper or shallower. If you can embrace the opportunity, you could really discover the character of him, the character of you and the character of your relationship. So instead of hiding out when you're feeling down with PMS or a bad day at work, this may be a good opportunity to see if he's there for you, a real chance to build the relationship around something other than just a state of feeling good.

Learning in the "Laser Lane"

If you want to get past the flash and into the substance of your guy and you want to do it fast, these are the lines of questioning and observations that will get you there. Once you know what to ask and watch out for, you can cut down the time it takes to get to know someone and build a foundation for a relationship more quickly than you've ever done before—and better than you ever could have imagined.

Mindless pleasantries, small talk and superficial chitchat are useless, and while it is not possible to eliminate this chatter

Be Natural

A word of advice: Now that you've got your questions and know what to look for, do not show up at your next date with a laundry list in hand. This is not your big chance to play Barbara Walters. It's not about making a grown man cry or sending the poor guy home with a third-degree burn. If he thinks he's taking an oral exam, he'll just tell you what he thinks you want to hear. So use finesse and, above all, be natural.

How you ask the questions is just as important as the questions themselves. If what you're after is the actual truth and not some cock-and-bull story your date has concocted to get you off of his back and onto yours, you'll need these tips:

- Talk about yourself: Tell him about something light that's going on at work or with your family. Then stop and say, "But enough about me. What's going on at your job?" Or, "Tell me about your family." The guy will be happy to have his chance to speak.
- Show vulnerability: According to the laws of reciprocity, if you reveal a mistake you made in your life, your date is more likely to open up about his own transgressions.
- Ask naturally, as the situations present themselves. These questions are meant to be peppered throughout your conversation across time, not asked all at once.
- After you ask, be quiet and listen: Many of you probably feel uncomfortable with silence and have a ten-

dency to fill in the blanks with rambling—maybe even to answer the question for yourself. Resist this impulse at all costs.

altogether, it should be minimized. Not only will talking about things that matter advance the relationship at a record pace, but it will distinguish you in his mind as a substantive individual. If you are tired of wasting effort and energy, now is the time to go deep and create velocity in your love life. These questions are about opening up meaningful topics and finding out which men qualify for your agenda. Once the guy is talking to you about his childhood, you've defined the relationship at a level of intimacy that will prove to be a positive development. You're finding out intimate details about his life. He's not sitting there trying to impress you with his cars and his clothes and his VIP passes to the Dave Matthews concert. Instead, he is feeling that you're getting to know the real him. And you are. What you do with that information is up to you.

Everybody including you likes to talk about himself or herself, but you need to resist doing too much of that for the time being and focus on learning about him instead. And if you will listen, just listen, not only will he tell you exactly how to close the deal but will help you figure out whether it's a deal you want to make in the first place.

10

Bag 'em, Tag 'em, Take 'em Home

If women ran the world we wouldn't have wars, just intense negotiations every 28 days.

ROBIN WILLIAMS

Okay, here's the chapter where you cash in your chips. The one you've been waiting for on how to reel him in. You've found a guy who you think is the one. Well, maybe not the One, but at least someone in the top five! Someone you don't want to erase from your radar screen, speed dial, address book and memory cells in your brain. You're thinking, "You know what? This one could work. I could see myself hanging with him for a while, maybe a long while. He's certainly a good enough candidate to put some effort into." Or maybe you're even further down the relationship road and are ready to have that Talk about being exclusive and calling him your boyfriend. Perhaps you've been there, done that and already have your names on the same mailbox and your toothbrushes mingling in the toothbrush holder. Now it seems time to step up and close the deal, get "the fish in the boat," walk down the aisle, tie the knot, whatever you want to call it. The point is, wherever you are with this guy, you want to get to the next level. You want to move things along and invest even more in this relationship and—more important—cause him to invest in you.

If it is really getting serious, more toward the "fish in the boat" end of the continuum, let's stop right here and do an extra gut check where you honestly ask yourself, "Is this guy Mr. Right or is he just Mr. Right Now?" Sure, today you're head over heels (or at least you think you are) and this guy is perfect (or at least you think he is). Well, let's just make sure you're doing this for the right reasons—because the worst thing that can happen is that you close the deal, walk down the aisle, take that Hawaiian honeymoon and then get this guy home, get him "unwrapped" and then the newness kind of wears off. You think, "Uh-oh! Is this the same guy? Was there a mix-up at security at the airport? Has he mutated from Mr. Wonderful into Mr. What Was I Thinking? This guy doesn't look right. He doesn't feel right. I'm not so sure he even smells right." Well, that could happen if you were seeing him through the "looove filter" instead of through clear eyes. Or you could have been fooled by your desperation. One of the worst things you can do is pick some guy not because you're attracted to him, but because you are repelled by your current life. You don't ever want to get married or committed to a relationship because you're moving away from something instead of toward something. Those kinds of mistakes in judgment are exactly what I want to help you prevent right now. So let me give you some don'ts:

- Don't move a relationship to the next level of commitment or marriage thinking that flaws, fallacies and fundamental incompatibilities you are experiencing on a part-time basis will be fixed by moving the relationship forward. Walking down the aisle, filling out paperwork and registering with the county won't fix what ails your relationship. If you have part-time problems in a part-time relationship, you're going to have full-time problems in a full-time relationship. Think of it this way: The quirks you force yourself to overlook when you're dating will gnaw at you like a tick on a dog when you're togther full-time. If you're already married and have problems, then you do have to work to fix them. But you don't have to volunteer.

- Don't think that things will get better once you're living together and married. The problems you have now won't go away just because you've got a ring on your finger.
- Don't think that you can live with the problems in your relationship because other parts of your lives will compensate for it, or make it worthwhile, such as being able to say you're married, having kids or buying a home.

- Don't think of marriage as one long extended date. Sure, now when you see him, he's got his best foot forward. He's always got plenty of gel in his hair and a clean shirt on. Believe me, that's not what he looks like on Sunday morning once the "new" has worn off the relationship. There is a huge difference between "being" in love and "falling" in love. There's an even a bigger difference between being in love and just wishing you were. There's an even a bigger difference yet in being in a relationship with a man who is simply not who you wish he was.

The bottom line: If it's wrong now, it's only going to get worse after you fill out the paperwork on this boy and get him home. So don't con yourself.

So once you've done your own gut check and you've decided you're good and ready, how do you know if he's feeling the same way? Let's face it, many men simply don't put on their jogging shoes and run to make a commitment. Some guys' idea of a serious commitment is that they will stay the entire night. You know what I'm talking about: You'll start talking about long-term commitment, and he'll start acting as nervous as a long-tailed cat in a room full of rocking chairs. As you seek to overcome this skittishness, pay very close attention to how he responds not only to what you do but also to the march of progress, or lack thereof, in the relationship. I say this because a man's position on something as serious as commitment will express itself in many different ways, and signs of commitment or—just as important—signs of a lack of commitment can sometimes take really unusual forms.

As a case in point, one of my threshold moments concerning my commitment to Robin when we were dating, was expressed in a very unusual form, which may have been entirely missed by Robin. She and I had been dating for a good while. I was really enjoying it but certainly had not given much, if any, thought to a long-term commitment. We, or at least I, weren't really serious or not serious. Seriousness just wasn't an issue. We were just having a good time. (Famous last words!) Then one night on a date Robin did something that really upset me. (It was so profound that I can't even remember what it was, but the point is that it was important at the time.) I was really bummed about it. But I quickly decided that I didn't have the right to say anything about it because we weren't yet in any kind of a long-term relationship. If you're not invested in a relationship and you don't see it going forward on any kind of permanent basis, then why worry about fixing tomorrow? It's like making plans to renovate a house that's not yours.

So, being "Mr. Noncommitted," I bit my tongue and just hopped into my car and off I went. But before I'd gotten even a mile down the road it was like a lightbulb going off. I realized I actually did care about this girl. I did want to go to that next step. I did believe that I wanted this relationship to move forward. And faster than you can say, "Who would of thunk it?" I turned that car around, found Robin and told her just what I had on my mind. We talked it through and resolved it.

The point is that people in general and guys in particular can show commitment in a million different ways. This was one of my ways of actually moving to the next level. She may have thought it was just a disagreement, but for me it was a watershed event. I was saying, "I want to put my energy and emotions into you and this relationship and move forward with you." (I know, I know—she was probably reeling me in like a widemouth bass.) So stay alert and watch for cues however subtle or nontraditional they may be.

I hope you haven't been jumping around and skipping forward in the book, because a lot of things we've talked about so far are important and are going to come into play now. I talked about the 80 percent solution back in Chapter 2, and here's where we've got to put it into action to figure out if this guy's got the 80 percent of what you want to move this thing along the relationship spectrum.

The key here is ask yourself, "Do I know enough to see if this guy's got 80 percent of what I want?" Here's how to find out. Look at these key areas and see what he's got and what he doesn't. Remember, it's okay if he doesn't have them all (that's the 20 percent and we'll chat about that later). And, as

I said earlier, no one is going to ever add up to 100 percent. If you expect him to be perfect, you're fooling yourself. So ask yourself the questions in Chapter 2 and answer honestly. (No one else is going to see your responses. This is between you and you.)

Okay, so you've asked yourself the appropriate questions and your guy comes up short of 80 percent. That doesn't mean it's time to toss him like last month's *TV Guide*. You've just got to iron out your lingering concerns and see if he can take some baby steps to up his score. He doesn't have to be there now, he just has to have the potential to move forward. Back in Chapter 9, I gave you lots of questions for assessing a guy in the early stages of dating. Now you're making a decision about a life partner, so it's time to take a much closer, more serious look at him. Now, all of a sudden, it could get real. You are going to a new level, so you have to measure him differently. It's like house hunting. First, you look at ten houses. Then you say, "Now, since this is the house I will likely live in for the next ten years, I'm going to look at it again." Then you go back and take a closer, more serious look, evaluating whether you could live there or not.

That's what you're doing here. To accomplish this, you've got to set up opportunities for him to show you. Remember that actions speak much louder than words. He can talk a good game, but if you set up situations to observe him and don't necessarily tell him that they are tests, your observations are going to be worth far more than any ring he might get you. What you have to do is be mindful of what kind of data you're going after and pay close attention to even subtle clues.

For example, let's say that spirituality tops your list of important traits. Well, then, don't just ask his opinion on the subject; invite him to church or temple with you. If he rolls his eyes, says no or goes but spends the whole time asking when you can leave, you'll know where he stands and how close the two of you are at least on the religion part of spirituality. Ask him to pray with you without getting into a preachy discussion about faith with him, and watch his reactions.

If his being comfortable with the emotional side of life is a biggie for you, then give him a chance to strut his emotional stuff. Call him when you're flipping out about that run-in with your boss and see how he responds. Does he sit on the phone, listen as you vent and talk it through with you? Does he come over ASAP? (Give him extra points for bringing your favorite comfort food.) Or does he interrupt you midsentence to tell you he's in the middle of something and will get back to you later? Maybe affection is key to you. Test him by reaching across the table during dinner to see if he holds your hand. Snuggle up to him or brush your hand across his knee and see how he responds. Does he stiffen up or move closer to you? To find out if you both have the same definition of joy, rent your favorite comedy and notice if he laughs along. Do something silly and check out his reaction—whether it's dancing in the kitchen while you're fixing lunch or singing along with the car radio (even though you're no Sheryl Crow). Does he tell you to grow up or does he sing along? If having children is important to you, babysit for your nephew or a friend's kid with him. Does he get down on the floor and play with the child or does he keep asking you when the parents will be home? Maybe a social man is a must-have.

Invite him to your next family gathering. Does he talk to your family members and make an effort to get to know them or does he become a mute? Ask to tag along on just one of his "boys' nights out." Is he proud to be by your side or does he dart off in the opposite direction and act standoffish?

By now you probably get what I'm talking about. I've given you a couple of good examples of elements that may be part of your 80 percent and you can do this in any area that you are unclear about. Make a list of these desires and set up similar test situations so you can observe how he acts. (He may even be doing the same for you!) Remember, your definition of 80 percent is unique and personal and there's no right or wrong. Anything that's important to you should go on the list. But I suggest that you give some thought to clarifying where he stands on such important issues as family, children, in-laws, sex, career, money and division of labor.

Remember that he may not respond the way you want him to or he may respond well but clumsily. That's okay; at least he's behaving in the category of functioning that you're looking for. There is a lot to be said for being a willing spirit. Don't obsess over the words and instead notice the actions. Does he try to comfort you? Make you feel better? Even if it's not the exact reaction you want, is it in the ballpark? (And if you're waiting for the exact reaction you have in your head, forget it. You'll be waiting a long time, since no one is a mind reader.) Again, it's that old saying: Actions speak louder than words.

What about the 20 percent that misses the mark? Good question. You've got to take a hard look at that, too, to get some clues as to whether you should stay or go when it comes to this relationship. Like I've said before, there are a few things that are deal breakers—things that are exempt from the 20 percent rule. These include addictions—to drugs, alcohol, gambling—infidelity, dishonesty, a violent temper and physical or verbal abuse.

As for the rest of the 20 percent, these can be things that you can work on later (being a bad dresser or not replacing the toilet-paper roll, for example) or that you don't love about him but can deal with (he hates sports while you never miss the home team's games). Believe me, you'll never love everything about someone. If you think you do, then you're wearing rose-colored RayBans and fooling yourself. And you don't have to like exactly the same things, or you'll be bored to tears. You don't want to be married to yourself: to somebody who thinks like you, looks like you, feels like you. You want to be married to someone with his own personality, interests and way of being in this world. If after taking this kind of hard look at your guy, you find that he doesn't measure up, what then? It's time to make a break. Be honest with yourself. If it's not right, you're just burning daylight. One thing worse than being in a bad relationship for six months is being in a bad relationship for six months and one day.

! Warning Signs

If you see any of the following signs, don't go a step further. Bells should be going off, because these are deal breakers. Hit the eject button immediately and parachute to safety.

- ✔ He drinks too much or is an alcoholic or drug addict.
- ✔ He's abusive—physically or verbally.
- ✔ He's got a bad temper.
- ✔ He's overly jealous.
- ✔ He's dishonest.
- ✔ He's controlling. He tells you how to dress and who to hang out with.
- ✔ He has a gambling addiction.
- ✔ He says he "can't live without you" after just two dates.
- ✔ He's thirty-five or older and still lives with his parents.
- ✔ He says he's "not technically, legally single. But we've been separated a long time."

- ✔ He doesn't make eye contact when he's talking to you.
- ✔ He doesn't introduce you to other people when you're out with him.
- ✔ He isn't there for you in times of crisis.

Power Tools for Closing the Deal

There are certain tools, techniques and interaction styles that, when used properly, can greatly influence a man's behavior. You may like these, and you may not. You may think they are manipulative and controlling. If so, don't use them. But whether they are right, wrong or indifferent, my point is that they are powerful in influencing what your man does or doesn't do. This is negotiation, and it's how you'll get the deal closed.

Here's how.

Enter the negotiation with a spirit of giving. To be a good negotiator, you need to figure out what your guy wants and focus on these things just as much as you focus on what you want. The first rule of negotiation for me, certainly in relationships, is asking myself, "How can I get the other person the most of what he or she wants?" It's like going back to when you negotiated your curfew with your parents. You made a mistake if you thought what they wanted was you home at 12 P.M. What they *really* wanted was to know whether you were safe or not. A lot of kids argued about the time they got home. I argued about whether I was safe or not because that was what was important to my parents.

Identify his desires. Here, you have to look hard to find out what he *really* wants. Then you have to decide whether those are things that you can and will bring to your relationship. For example, say your guy's been in relationships where he's been burned and is skeptical about a woman's ability to be honest, faithful and trustworthy. In that case, his top priority is not day-to-day companionship or sex; it's fidelity. That's the most important thing to him. Your first response might be to say, "No problem. I'll just tell him that I will never cheat on him or hurt him. I'll promise." But that's what the last girl said. That promise is necessary, but not sufficient. This guy has been betrayed, he is hurting and he is afraid. More powerful than a promise is communicating this to him: "I get what happened to you. I get what it did to you. It's terrible and I want to help heal that wound for you." You don't think he is being silly and you don't think it's wrong.

He wants a woman who understands how important fidelity is to him and how critical it is to him, and you need to tell him you are prepared to make this a priority. He has a big fear and he will never get over that fear unless and until he understands that you get it and that he has been heard. You've got to make a pledge to him and say, "If I don't want to be in the relationship, I won't cheat on you. Instead, I'll tell you flat out that it's not working. You don't have worry that I'm doing something I shouldn't do. I will tell you. I get it. I get it." Once he knows this, you will have a better chance of negotiating.

This is just one example of what I'm talking about, but it's true of a lot of situations. He has to know that you understand him, that you know what is truly important to him and want to make this a priority. In some cases, you may not be willing to do this. Say you take a hard look at your guy and realize that what he wants is a woman who is subservient, who does what he says and doesn't ask questions when he comes home at 2 A.M.—a woman who "knows her place." If this is the case and you aren't willing to meet these needs, then either he moves his position or the game's over.

Back to Basics

We all have needs, and part of a relationship and wanting to be close to someone is that this person fulfills these needs. It would seem there are seven basic categories of needs.

- Survival: What do you have that helps him survive and live better? One guy I know said he was attracted to his wife because she had her household established. He liked joining the party instead of having to blow up the balloons and hang the streamers.

- Security: He wants to know that you'll be loyal to him, that you won't cheat on him. He wants know he's got a soft place to fall.
- Affection: He wants to be shown love in various ways, from simply rubbing his back to sex.
- Self-esteem: He wants to know you're proud of him.
- Acknowledgment: He wants to be heard and to know that you value his opinion.
- Smart enough: He wants to know that you have faith in him.
- Purpose in life: He wants you to help him do something that's bigger than himself, that makes him feel he's adding to the welfare of the world.

Soothe his fears. Any time you are trying to close a deal the other side is going to have objections and obstacles. The primary obstacle you'll have with men is a prominent fear or discomfort with the unknown. Men in particular like to feel they are in control and that their life is predictable, especially with regard to financial security. Unknowns and ambiguity can be unsettling to them. They wonder, "How will this work? Where would we live? How much money would we have? What would we do about cars, holidays, family, kids?" You've got to allay his fears of the unknown. Recognize them and address them.

Make your compromises clear. Another one of his concerns is the cost of affiliation, and compromise in all areas of his life to be with you. In plain language it boils down to him wondering, "All right—I want her, but what's it going to cost me? What do I have to give up? I love my sports car, playing in two softball leagues and fly-fishing every Saturday. I love the duck-hunting trip my buddies and I have been taking every year for the last fifteen years. What am I going to have to give up to get what I get?" This is a big deal to a guy. To get him comfortable with this cost of compromise, be clear about what he has to give up to meet your needs.

Be honest here. Don't bait and switch and say, "Oh, I'm fine with golf every Saturday. No problem." Don't say that if it isn't what you think and feel. You have to give him as much of what he wants as you can truly live with—not any more than that. You don't want to close the deal and realize it wasn't what you wanted.

Create urgency. Every rocket needs fuel, and the fuel that will accelerate this negotiation forward is urgency. I've said it before: Most men aren't commitment-phobic; they're simply not likely to experience the same level of urgency that you might be feeling. It's not that they don't want to partner with you for the long term, it's that sometimes they just don't recognize a good reason to do it right now. The problem is summed up in an old saying: "Why buy the cow if you can get the milk for free?" Research confirms this attitude.

According to The National Marriage Report at Rutgers University, the number-one reason men don't commit is that they know they can get sex without getting married.

You're going to have to play a little poker. I mean you've got to know when to hold 'em and know when to fold 'em. It is a gamble to know when to withhold part of yourself. You're probably thinking, "But if I don't give him what he wants, there are lots of other girls who will. Then what's his incentive to stay?" That may apply to in terms of who his date is at the lake this weekend, but it is not true when it comes to who he wants to marry or have a committed relationship with. If marriage or a committed relationship is what you want, you'd better hold 'em instead of fold 'em. The risk/reward ratio is in your favor when it comes to a long-term relationship.

You've heard me talk about the fact that

there needs to be some mystery, some intrigue. You can be affectionate, you can be warm, you can be physical, but if you leave nothing to the imagination, if there is no motivation for him to take your relationship to the next level, he has absolutely no urgency. What could the guy who has everything possibly want? To start sharing a laundry basket with you? I can assure you that is not what lights a guy up. You have to hold something in reserve for the ultimate level of your relationship or he will be much less motivated to move there. There are several things that you can and should hold in reserve until he's willing to make the ultimate commitment, and sex would be on the short list of those things held in reserve. To repeat: Since most sexual partners don't wind up marrying you it isn't even right to call it premarital sex, it is just sex! So don't kid yourself. I'm not trying to be prudish here; I'm just telling you how guys think and how this works. Whether this appeals to your morality or whether it appeals to your greed, just recognize that if there is absolutely nothing that he doesn't know about you, share with you, experience with you, he will have no reason to commit to you.

What's another thing you can hold in reserve? His access privileges. It's that caveman mentality I mentioned in Chapter 6: Men's behaviors change when they've got a little competition. It will be highly effective to let him know without a doubt that he is not the only game in town. This doesn't mean getting another boyfriend, but it does mean becoming less available to him. If you're totally accessible 24/7 and there's never any question that you're sitting at home on call for him, then you are too easy—and to him, you're liking playing basketball with eight-foot-high hoops. A guy will not be moved by a girl who's always available. He needs to understand that if he snoozes, he darn sure loses.

How do you make yourself unavailable? Invest your time in activities that you've always wanted to take up but never had the chance to do. Volunteer one night a week, or take that art class, or stay later at work to get even closer to that promotion. By being unavailable and not just sitting there waiting for him, you give yourself some value and more than a little power. Don't bluff; really do get busy. It's the old notion of the thrill of the chase. Sometimes men need that chase to see how much they really want you and to be pushed to some action. Men are competitive beings. If a man knows, "I've got her," there is no intrigue here, there's no mystery here—he will not value you as much as otherwise. You want him to know that your calendar isn't just wide open for him. You're a busy woman on the go. You have to be the pursued, not the pursuer. He will not pursue you with any sense of urgency if he believes he has this in the bag. You can't let him take you for granted.

Why Men Won't Commit to Marriage

According to *The National Marriage Report* at Rutgers University, here are the top ten reasons that men don't want to marry.

1. *They can get sex without marriage more easily today than in times past.*

2. They can enjoy the benefits of having a wife by cohabiting rather than marrying.
3. They want to avoid divorce and its financial risks.
4. They want to wait until they are older to have children.
5. They fear that marriage will require too many changes and compromises.
6. They are waiting for the perfect soul mate, and she hasn't yet appeared.
7. They face few social pressures to marry.
8. They are reluctant to marry a woman who already has children.
9. They want to own a house before they get a wife.
10. They want to enjoy single life as long as they can.

Tell him where you stand. Another way to get him to commit is to declare your position in the relationship and then let him meet you if he wants. This builds his urgency (and if it doesn't, well, then, there's your answer and he's not the guy for you). Now this isn't an ultimatum—nobody responds to ultimatums—this is declaring your position. There's a difference. An ultimatum is saying, "If you don't do A, I'm doing B." Declaring your position is saying, "I'm at a point where I'm going to do B." And if he wants to do something about it he can. But again, when you say that, you can't be bluffing. Be prepared to move on.

Setting the Foundation

Now you know how to negotiate for what you want, find out what he needs and weigh this against what you can and want to fulfill. You know how to express your needs and see where he stands. You know what he's willing to give and not give. Does that work for you? Make sure. This isn't about telling someone what he wants to hear (or hearing only what you want to hear from him). No matter how good you are at negotiating, you don't want to close the deal and realize that what you got isn't what you want. Even if you kept the receipt, returning him won't be easy. Your goal is to create a relationship that is good for both of you, where both of you feel safe, both of you feel your needs are met and both of you feel that the things you've compromised on are worth it because of what you get in return. If that's the case, then you've got the foundation in place for this relationship. Keep building on it.

11

The State of Your Union

If a man becomes everything a woman thinks she wants him to become, she probably wouldn't like him at all.

DR. PHIL MCGRAW

I said earlier that there is a difference between falling in love and being in love. Think about it. When you are falling in love everything he does is cute, funny and interesting. It's amazing how connected the two of you are. You can read each other's minds, you can stay up all night just talking and you are so astoundingly synchronized that you can even finish each other's sentences. Ahhh, the starry-eyed early days. Having that 24/7 happens only in the movies, where a lifetime is lived in just two hours. Floating on that romantic high feels great, but if living on a cloud like that were even a taste of reality, our country's legions of divorce lawyers would be out of work. Eventually you will wake up from that dizzy, I-can't-stop-talking-about-him whirlwind and plant your feet back on the ground. A few months later, when you're in love, as opposed to falling in love, it can feel a whole lot different. At first you couldn't bear to be away from each other, he always greeted you with a kiss and your heart raced just at the thought of him. Now you value your private time. It used to be so cute that he could finish your sentences and now it's, "Hey, buddy, quit interrupting me!"

Does that mean you're no longer in love and maybe never were? Absolutely not. It just means that sometimes the thrill and excitement, the exhilaration and electricity of a new love can transform into a more comfortable, predictable and secure love. It's not better; it's not worse; it's just different. Life happens. You have kids, switch jobs, have an illness or death in your immediate or extended family, become empty nesters, retire, etc. Other things also have an impact: for example, a physical change (one of you gains or loses lots of weight) as well as spiritual changes (one of you converts). There are lots of other scenarios, but you get the point. Love can and does change, but there are definite upsides to the more comfortable, less electrifying love. You always have a date on Friday nights. You have someone to check in with daily and someone who is waiting for you when you get home and who will start to worry if you don't arrive on time. You're lucky enough to have regular sex with one person you love. The list goes on and on.

Hopefully that comfortable and predictable love will be punctuated by moments, days or even longer periods of the initial electricity. But there is a difference, nonetheless. What we're talking about now is when that comfortable love becomes too comfortable and slips into a lackadaisical, apathetic existence in which the focus is no longer on the quality of the relationship. Children, money problems, careers, hobbies, in-laws and just the sameness, day after day after day, can erode that which makes the relationship work and worth having. When that happens your fires just need some rekindling. You have reached a stage where you are now taking each other or your relationship for granted. So whether you're currently stuck in a rut or just want to prevent one and keep the fires burning strong, read on.

But don't freak out, not yet. Don't work yourself into a frenzy because things aren't the way they were in those hormone-fueled early days. You haven't necessarily made a horrible mistake, and a trip to divorce court (or a breakup) is not necessarily right around the corner. Don't worry that something is terribly wrong.

When you date long term, move in together or get married, it's natural that things are going to change.

That's because when you merge two lives (not to mention two CD collections) it's a challenge. You're sharing space, time, money, effort, energy and labor. Compromises need to be made, and you see all sides of each other's personalities—not just the best foot you put forward in the beginning. You see the ugly stuff, too, and I'm not just talking about morning breath and what he looks like when he's got the flu. You see the moodiness, stress, sadness and anger—sometimes in one day. And that can be a good thing because if you're at this stage with someone and all you've ever seen is a smile on his face, then you're with a mannequin, not a man.

Reviving Your Relationship

Before you start reading all these things that I'm going to recommend doing, I want to tell you why I'm putting all the burden on you. You are the one reading this book right now. You are the only one I'm communicating with right now. I want you to accept the burden because you are the only one that you control. You can inspire your man, you can influence him, but you cannot control him.

The good news about changing a relationship is that both people don't have to be working on it at the same time for major changes to occur. Sure, it would be better if you were both working on it. But when your relationship stalls out, it doesn't matter who jump-starts it, just as long as someone does. Once things get better and you feel that you're back on track, you won't care who started it. If you begin making changes in the way you engage him, the way you conduct yourself, the way you live, the pattern of your life—and those changes are constructive—he is going to notice and very likely start responding differently.

One woman I know who ran a business from her house was always at the computer when her husband came home. She'd be hunched over her keyboard, would barely grunt "Hello" and never got up to greet him. Sometimes she'd work for a good hour or two before they were even in the same room. (No wonder they were in a relationship rut!) Then one day, she decided to actually get her butt out of that chair. When she heard him coming through the door, she actually got up, said hello, gave him a kiss, then she went back to work. She decided to do this regularly. Even though it took a mere few minutes and the smallest effort on her part, she said it changed her relationship. Just having that little bit of eye contact and interaction made her feel more connected to her husband. He obviously felt the same way, because he became warmer to her. He made an effort to do small things for her too. A few weeks later, the topic of her small gesture came up. He admitted that her getting up from the computer made him feel better. Instead of ignoring him, she acknowledged him. I'm not saying that suddenly they lived happily ever after because of a tiny gesture, but I am saying that someone's got to get the ball rolling—and when you do, you get a response.

Robin and I have a "four-minute rule." The minute I walk through the door at the end of the day, I go and find her, say hello and talk about our day. Those four minutes count. They set the tone for the rest of the evening. Try doing this with your guy. It will make a difference.

You really have a huge power to influence and change this relationship. There's no way that it's going to happen if you sit there waiting for him and he sits there waiting for you. This relationship needs a hero to step up and be the hero right now. Remember, the main thing is this: If what you're doing isn't working, change it. Sometimes the changes can be superficial and sometimes they have to be more meaty. As we go forward, I'm going to suggest a long list of action-oriented things for you and your partner to do. If he refuses to participate, that's okay; you just do it alone. There's a good chance he will come around. Again, this relationship needs a hero, and since you're the only one holding this book and since you're armed with some Guy-Q knowledge from Chapter 6, you get the job.

Some of you may be reading this section just to see how to keep the fires burning. Others are reading it because something doesn't seem right. You're thinking, "We were in love, but it has gone south. There's no fun, no passion and no energy. We're in an emotional divorce. We are just roommates."

When you're at that point, don't resign

yourself to thoughts like: "This is just how things are. I've got to accept it" or "Things are so bad. Why try to make them better?" Big mistake. You are meant to be happy, and your relationship can improve. It's not in an unchanging, permanent state, so don't give up on it. Make dealing with it a priority no matter what else you've got on your to-do list and no matter what else anyone thinks. In fact, the latter shouldn't play any role as you work on your relationship. Don't feel embarrassed in front of friends and family because your relationship has hit a speed bump. These people aren't the ones feeling sad and disconnected, so forget about them. Don't give up on the relationship, and don't simply walk out—literally and figuratively—without giving it your best shot and trying. That's a cop-out. Lastly, don't play games with your partner. Games don't do anything but make matters worse.

Games People Play

When things aren't going well, it's all too easy to act childish and toy with your partner. Trust me—that won't get you anywhere. Toying just makes you focus on your problems instead of figuring out how to make things better.

- Don't act mean-spirited and say things just to hurt him.
- Don't focus on finding fault with everything he does.
- Don't keep score of who did or didn't do what.
- Don't fight about unimportant things, like which way the toilet paper is put on the roll, to cover up the real issues.
- Don't make excuses like, "I have a headache; let's not talk about this tonight" or "I'm too depressed to deal with this."
- Don't get caught up in a sabotage group. These are friends who are

having similar problems with their mates, so you complain to each other. Since these complaints hold your group together, you fear changing because you'll lose your seat at the party.

As I said earlier, you can start to work on your relationship and make changes without getting your partner involved. I once asked a woman who was married over fifty years what her secret was. "My husband and I never fell out of love at the same time," she said. "There were times when I wasn't feeling it and he carried us through and vice versa. But now we're happier than we were on the day we met." My point here is that you and your partner don't always have to be on the same page at all times to have a loving, secure, healthy relationship. I believe that you get what you give. If you change the way you are in the relationship, you'll change the way he responds. So create what you want. Wake up every morning and ask yourself:

"What can I do to make my relationship more loving? To amp up the energy? To reignite that spark?" Instead of complaining about the flowers you're not getting or hoping that he'll go back to being the charming guy he used to be, get the ball rolling by doing little things to show him you love him. These small things will be appreciated and reciprocated. Decide what you want. If you want new activities in your relationship, make a list of what those are and then add them to your life. If you want more of a social life, an interesting hobby, travel or any other new experience, identify exactly what it is and then make a plan for getting it. If you want more excitement in the bedroom, think about what that means to you and create it. Make time for it.

The Formula for Lasting Love

When both people in a relationship get their needs met, then that relationship is going to be successful. But there's not a soul on earth who can meet your needs if you don't have a clue what they are. Finding out takes some self-exploration (like what we did in

Chapter 3). You also have to know firmly what you value in him and what will fulfill you (which we talked about in Chapter 2). Is it important that your mate is proud of you? That you're respected and valued? That you're desired? Be honest about what your emotional, physical, spiritual and social needs are, and don't feel compelled to justify any of them. They're not right or wrong. They are what they are, and getting real about them is a crucial first step to giving your guy a shot at loving you the way you want to be loved.

Once you've figured out what you want, ask him for it and tell him why something is important to you. Don't assume he knows the answer. Things don't have the same meaning for each of you. For example, when he takes out the garbage or clears the table, you feel that he respects you. I can bet that to him taking out the garbage is just taking out the garbage and doing dishes is just doing dishes. He hasn't a clue that there's deeper meaning. Spell it out for him, because honestly men don't get it. Men aren't that bright when it comes to this stuff. You'd think that saying something like "The fact that we don't talk about anything real is hurting me" would make a difference and show your guy that he needs to be more genuine, feeling and forthcoming. But most men won't get there. And if you think that you shouldn't have to tell him at all, then you've been reading too many romance novels. Your partner's not a mind reader; and until you can be clear about what you want, it's difficult for him to address what you're after. He's left guessing or lost—not a great strategy for a relationship. You may think he's insensitive or rude, but this may be simply because he doesn't know your needs.

Don't think that it doesn't count if you have to tell your partner what he should do to make you happy. Loving, caring, considerate actions can still be meaningful and come from his heart even if they weren't his idea. Who cares whose idea they were if your need for affection or respect is being met the way you want it to be? Stop complaining about what you don't want and start asking, very specifically, for what you do want. Don't say, "I don't want you to play golf every Saturday." Instead, tell him, "I want you to spend two Saturdays a month with me and the kids, and then you can play golf on the other two." Tell him something with a verb in it, and he will do a whole lot better. Put your fears aside and express your expectations. When he does things the way you'd like, make sure you praise him. Let him know that what he's doing is making you feel good. For example, if he takes out the garbage and you say, "It's about time you did that. You've finally pulled yourself away from the game long enough to help me," his helpfulness will last about two minutes and it's highly unlikely he'll be taking out the trash again soon. But if you give things a positive spin by saying, "Thank you. It really means a lot to me when you help," chances are you won't have to put up with any garbage again—literally or figuratively.

Strive to do the same for him. I talk about discovering the most private parts of your partner's soul. Once you have discovered them, and you know things about him that few others know, consider what you can do for him that no one else can. How can you support him? Protect him? Help him feel complete and happy?

Part of the challenge here is that many men believe that relying on other people, especially emotionally, is a sign of weakness; but until a man can get honest about the fact that he has needs, and then figure out what they are, it will be very difficult for him to be intimate with you.

Explain that it's important to you to feel needed, but use language that's easy on him. Instead of saying, "What do you need from me?" try "What do you value from me? What is it that I do or say that's most important to you?"

Whether or not they admit it to themselves or their partners, many men want desperately to hear that their wives are proud of them. I know I do. I get plenty of validation from viewers and readers, but that pales in comparison to knowing that my wife is proud of who I am and what I do. Until we discussed her pride, she could not have understood how much this means to me. It may be hard to get your partner to tell you specifically what he needs; in that case just offer your general support. If he's like many men I've talked to, the best way to make him feel good about himself as a boyfriend or husband, father, provider and man is to tell him that he's doing a great job in all these capacities.

Good communication is a crucial part of keeping your relationship strong. Part of developing good communication skills is learning to listen. You want your guy to feel safe telling you anything. It's hard enough to get guys to talk; but if you make them feel secure and protected, certain that they can say what they want without being judged or attacked, they actually will open up. Show empathy. Be sincere and genuine. You want him to feel that he can share his deepest thoughts and concerns without feeling bad or ashamed. For women, it's natural to open up and share problems or emotions with other people. In fact, you may have a group of gal pals that you can regularly open up to. Guys just aren't like that. They don't reveal themselves to many people. They don't e-mail their best friend to talk about what's bothering them or meet for coffee to have a good cry. So you need to make yourself the person he can do that with. Believe me, when he feels this way about you, your connection will be solid. You'll be his cocoon, his soft place to fall—and there's nothing more comforting than that. You want to be his safe haven against all the stressful stuff that the rest of the world—his boss, job, family and friends—may heap on him. With you he shouldn't have to think about that stuff. And when you do talk about difficult issues, focus on the present. Don't dig up old wounds or spout off a list of all the things he's done wrong during the last year. Don't attack him when he talks. Show him that what he's telling you now won't be used against him later.

Here's one way to start talking and sharing more with each other. Start a routine of writing love letters. Once a week, you each write each other a letter. Spend no more than ten minutes on it. The topic can be anything you want, from how much fun you had this weekend going apple picking to something he said that hurt your feelings. Next, exchange letters with your partner. Say he gives you his letter. You have to read it and then tell him out loud what you think you read by saying, "What I think your letter said was . . . ," then fill in the blank. By doing this you make sure you're reading what he intended. It may sound silly, but often our interpretation is not the same as what the other person meant. After that, he gets a chance to respond out loud to what you said. This discussion part should go on for twenty minutes at the most. (Do this with each of your letters.) The whole process shouldn't take very long, but it will bring you closer. You'll talk about topics you wouldn't otherwise. You'll really listen to each other. It also makes you set aside time to be together. It helps ward off potential problems. It's like weighing yourself each week. If you do that, you'll know when you've gained a pound or two and then can do something about it. If you put it off for months, ten pounds may creep on without you noticing, and losing ten is much harder than losing two.

With weekly talking, small problems don't get left to snowball into something big. Not that all you're talking about is problems. Again, topics can be good, bad or neutral. One of the biggest mistakes couples make is to have meaningful conversations only when they're in crisis mode. But the love letter routine makes you take the time during peaceful moments that are free of distraction. Do this, and I promise that the way you two communicate in general will benefit. And so will your relationship. The more strange and unnatural this sounds or feels if you try it, the more you need to do it. If you wonder whether or not real people actually do this kind of thing, the answer is yes!

Reconnection Flow Chart

No matter what your personal situation is with your partner, you can generally follow the same strategy for reconnecting that will lead to a win-win result. Here are the specific steps.

1. Open the reconnection dialogue.
2. Describe the work you've been doing to reconnect.
3. Talk about the top relationship myths that you will find later in this chapter.

4. Share the formula for success in a relationship.
5. Clarify your partner's needs.
6. Share your own personal needs and fears.

Maintaining a Successful Relationship

Here are some other important, action-oriented ways to strengthen the bond between you and your partner.

- **Work on your relationship regularly.** I think it's funny that people spend time and money regularly fixing their cars, sprucing up their homes and hitting the gym to stay in shape, but when it comes to their relationship they think it can just coast along on cruise control. Do that and you're bound to be headed for a ditch. Remember when you played sports or were in a club in high school? That took a lot of commitment and hard work. The same energy and effort should go into your significant other. You can't focus on your relationship only when things are bad. You may have already planted the seeds of true love when you met and over the time you've been together. But if you don't tend to the garden, it will soon be consumed by weeds.

- **Don't take each other for granted.** He calls you during lunch, and instead of saying hello you rattle off a list of all the problems of the day: your boss was a jerk, the cat ran away, the kids got permanent marker on the couch. Or you use the bathroom with the door open and burp at the table. Or instead of thanking him for picking up your dry cleaning, you're asking him why he didn't do it yesterday. Some days you're nicer to the guy making your latte at Starbucks than you are to your own boyfriend or husband. The same thing happens on his end. My point is that there is a fine line between getting comfortable and getting careless. Crossing it can send a signal to your partner that you're taking him for granted and that you don't really care anymore. You don't have to be formal, but use the same manners with him as you would with a friend or coworker. Take the two minutes to say hello and good-bye when you greet each other or leave for the day.

- **Show each other you care.** In your dating days, you go out of your way to do sweet stuff for each other. He talks about how much he likes tennis and you beg, borrow and steal to get tickets to the U.S. Open. You mention that your favorite ice cream is rocky road and that night a pint awaits you in the freezer. It's little stuff, but it's little stuff that says a lot. That shouldn't change when you settle down. Showing your love means thinking about the small things you can do to improve each other's lives. Ask yourself how you can make his day better. Is there some way you can help him unwind when he's stressed? Make him feel loved, whether it's by sticking a sweet note in his shirt pocket to be found later or calling him at work just to say hi. Keep up the compliments. Tell him how good he looks in those jeans or what a great husband he is. It'll mean ten times more coming from you than from anyone else. Even something as mundane as brushing the snow off his windshield in the morning tells your mate that you want his life to be better and you'll make sacrifices to ensure that. If you do this kind of stuff, he'll want to return the favor. Just let him know what would work for you. Is it telling you to take a bath while he cleans up the kitchen? Or letting you sit and relax while he puts the kids to bed? Small gestures accumulate over time and create positive momentum in your relationship.

- ♥ **Don't forget about sex.** In the beginning, you can't stop thinking about having it, but when life gets busy, sex is one of the first casualties. This is a mistake. Besides the fact that you're missing out on something fun, you're also missing out on physical intimacy, which is a crucial part of any relationship. Sexuality is a pattern, something that needs to happen on an ongoing basis or else other things will crowd it out. Like the old adage: Use it or lose it, a scary thought, particularly to guys. Stop thinking of sex as a luxury and put it higher on your priority list. Being sexually satisfied and feeling wanted by your partner are legitimate and healthy parts of a relationship. Yes, sex changes as you're married. People change, and their needs change. What you enjoy now may be different from what you did when you first met your mate (the same goes for him). Talking about these things can keep your sex life satisfying.

- **Do your own thing.** This may sound contrary to what you think, because if you're happy you should be attached at the hip and eager to spend every waking moment together, right? Wrong. We all have things we enjoy that our partner doesn't—maybe you like skiing but he can't stand the cold or you're into art but he'd rather get his back waxed than go to a museum. The mistake we make is to give up our interests to appease our partners. In the beginning it may be okay, but at some point you're going to get bored and resent him. Doing everything together will eventually make you feel suffocated. You don't want to marry yourself. I've said it a million times: I don't want to be married to me. I don't want somebody who thinks the way I do, looks like me, feels the way I do. I want to be married to somebody who's got her own personality, her own interests, her own beliefs, her own way and style. Spending time apart focusing on your separate interests allows each of you to grow on your own. That growth will enhance your relationship when you're together.

- **Quit comparing.** Avoid comparing what you and your guy have with what your friend or sister has with her significant other: Your guy isn't as reliable as hers or as romantic as hers. They have a date night once a week and you don't. He talks so nicely to her. He surprised her with a watch for her birthday. It can go on and on, but the key here is this: You're comparing your reality with everybody else's social mask. There's no way you can win, because you're comparing apples and oranges. You know all the nitty-gritty about your relationship—the good, the bad and the ugly—and you're comparing it with only a fraction of your friend's relationship. You don't know the half of it. Remember the saying: You never know what happens behind closed doors. Think about all those stories on the news where the reporter interviews the neighbors of a guy who they just found out was a murderer or child molester. "He was such a nice guy. He was the perfect father, always playing ball with his kids. He was a deacon in his church. He always offered to mow my lawn." Well, they didn't know what was really going on. All they saw was the social persona, so remind yourself that this is all you're seeing of your friends' relationships, too.

- **Make life fun.** Sure stress, work, kids and bills come into play when you're in it for the long haul or married, but if you don't make time for each other and time for fun, excitement is just not going to happen. Be the initiator. Plan an evening out. Have more fun. Think about the things you did together in your early days as a couple that made life exciting. Did you go to sporting events or shows? Meet for lunch during the workday? Take long drives with no destination in mind? Whatever it was, try to incorporate those things back into your life.

Happy Couple Relationship Myths

Another thing that can chip away at a perfectly good relationship is believing all these myths about what a "happy" couple does or is. You believe these myths, and when your relationship doesn't measure up, you're convinced something's wrong.

MYTH: Happy couples can see things through each other's eyes.

REALITY: You can't possibly see things the same way as your mate, because you're just not the same people. You're different genetically, physically and psychologically and you've had different experiences in the world. You're a woman and he's a man, and you're not wired the same.

MYTH: Happy couples always have lots of romance.

REALITY: Most people confuse that giddy, dizzy feeling you have early on in your relationship with romance. Nope. That's called "infatuation" and it will pass. Romantic love is emotionally driven. It's novelty, excitement and newness, but it doesn't sustain a relationship.

MYTH: Happy couples can resolve all their disagreements.

REALITY: There are some basic issues that you will always disagree about. You each have your opinions on these things that won't change. Just agree to disagree.

MYTH: Happy couples need to have common interests.

REALITY: It's a bonus if you do, but there's nothing wrong with your relationship if you don't do the same activities. If you and your partner are forcing yourself to engage in common activities but the results are stress, tension and conflict, don't do it!

MYTH: Happy couples don't fight.

REALITY: Conflict is a fact of life in most relationships, and arguing—as long as it's not destructive and doesn't turn into character assassination—isn't a negative thing. Arguing can actually help the relationship by releasing tension and instilling the sense of peace and trust that comes from knowing that you can express feelings without being abandoned or humiliated. Plus, there's the make-up sex . . .

MYTH: Happy couples vent all their feelings to each other.

REALITY: Getting things off your chest might feel good, but when you blurt something out in the heat of the moment, you risk damaging your relationship permanently. Many relationships are destroyed when one partner can't forgive something that was said during uncensored venting.

Think before you say something you might regret.

MYTH: Being a happy couple has nothing to do with sex.

REALITY: A good sexual relationship can make you feel closer, more relaxed, more accepted and more involved with your partner. Keep sex on your list of priorities.

MYTH: Happy couples are always in sync sexually.

REALITY: Except maybe in the beginning when you can't keep your hands off each other, it's totally normal for you to be in the mood at different times.

MYTH: Happy couples know the right and wrong way to make their relationships great.

REALITY: There's no cookie-cutter way to be in a relationship, and no handbook on the proper way to love each other, fight, relate to each other or do anything else that has to do with being in a relationship. What's important is that your ways work for the two of you.

Relationships Are Managed, Not Cured

To keep your relationship on track, you have to realize that you and your partner are preprogrammed for conflict. You are trying to mesh your life with someone who is physically, mentally, emotionally and socially different from you. As a result, when differences arise, if you're not managing them with a great degree of awareness, then you're going to go spiraling right back down to the bottom. You've made advances, but never forget that you still must paddle upstream against the current for the rest of your life. You need to set goals and put a plan in place to keep your relationship healthy, to hang on to what you have worked so hard to gain.

The first trick to managing your new relationship is to pay close attention to your priorities. You must be driven to make your relationship outstanding. That is your priority. My rule is: If you catch yourself at any time doing something that is not in support of your priority or is antagonistic to it, stop what you are doing and change to something that is consistent with your priority.

The second task in managing your relationship is behaving your way to happiness. It sounds like a cliché, but to be great you must act great. You can move toward happiness simply by behaving in ways that define what happiness means to you in the relationship context. For example, if you like the way it feels when your partner looks at you and laughs or smiles, then do something that gives your partner the chance to look at you and smile. Create what you want by doing what you can. (For a more in-depth explanation of this, see my other book, *Relationship Rescue.*)

As part of reprogramming your relationship, you must have a particular plan to deal with what you know will be the weakest spot in your relationship. It could be fighting, withdrawal or getting stuck in your comfort zone. Whatever your trouble spot—

and I'm sure you already know what it is—you need to have "goals" and a plan in place to overcome these prominent weaknesses. For example, if lack of sex is a weakness in your relationship, then you must have a plan to change it. This could be as simple as initiating sex a set number of times per week. By the same token, you need similar goals and plans to build on the greatest strengths of your relationship. For example, if your time together on weekends is one of the most valuable parts of your life, then come up with goals to make sure you enhance the quality and quantity of those times together.

Next, you need to set goals and put a plan in place. All couples have enormous differences, and no amount of work can bridge that gap. As a result, you have to learn to manage your relationship despite the differences. What's more, you need to embrace them and find value in them. God didn't design men and women to be the same; he designed us to be different from each other. Look at your different views of a situation and your different ways of expressing thoughts as complementary attributes. Managing these differences does not mean that one partner should try to see a situation through the eyes of the other partner. It just means that being different is okay and should not be a source of frustration.

Lastly, there is admiration management. You've heard me say that if all you ever talk about is problems, then you have a problem relationship. If you dwell on what's wrong, it's easy to lose sight of what is right. If you dwell on the flaws and fallacies of your partner, it's easy to forget the admiration. You need a plan to remind yourself of all your partner's admirable qualities and remind yourself that a few bad tendencies doesn't cancel out everything else. Make a conscious commitment to nurture and develop your admiration for your partner. By becoming your partner's biggest fan, you will routinely choose to focus on those things about him that are unique and inspiring.

12

Live the Love You Feel

Great love happens in the blink of an eye. One moment you're enjoying your life, and the next you're wondering how you ever lived without them.

WILL SMITH, *HITCH*

When you picked up this book, you acknowledged that you wanted something in your life—something you did not have. The first thing I told you is that you'll never get what you want in this life unless you believe you deserve it. People holding a trophy may say the award should have gone to someone else, but they seldom give it away, and they shouldn't. They almost universally deserve it. That's why we spent so much time focused on these facts: You have to decide that you are fabulous, you have to decide that you are deserving and you have to embrace a positive personal truth. You have to fall in love with yourself before anyone else can fall in love with you. If, given the choice, you wouldn't hang with you, why should someone else? That's one reason why we gave your past relationships an autopsy. We needed to figure out what your relationship patterns were so we could do something to change the flow. We said that while we were going to identify a Character of Him, we were just as importantly going to focus on what the experience of you truly was.

Because I know you don't want to waste time, we focused on how to keep you from throwing away weeks or months with somebody who is not a genuine candidate. This is a very important learned skill. Basically, what I said is this: If you truly want to get the fish into the boat, you're going to have to fall in love with yourself and create what I call the "defined product." That is the specific configuration of your qualities, traits, characteristics and proclivities brought together in a way that deeply reflects who you are. Trying to be somebody you're not or trying to be all things to all people will leave you so lost and confused that even OnStar wouldn't help you; it's nothing more than an unnecessary detour on the road to love. You don't need to try to be somebody else, you don't need to pretend that you're interested in things that you're not, because there are a lot of guys out there who will be interested in you once they get to know you. They'll be drawn to you once they can recognize how passionate and excited you are about life.

That's all good philosophy, but I also wanted to give you important specific skills you needed to get into the game and actually make it happen. That was crucial because I wanted you to know what actions you needed to take in order to create the results that you wanted. I'm a longtime believer in the formula BE-DO-HAVE.

BE committed to what you want;
DO what it takes to get it and you will
HAVE what it is that you want.

That's true in any area of your life, especially your love life, and I wanted to give you specific steps and actions necessary to redefine yourself in the social arena. I don't want you wasting time, and I know that you feel your biological clock is ticking loudly enough to wake the dog next door. I felt it was important to give you the skills necessary to make a determination about a guy fairly early on in a relationship as opposed to burning six or eight months only to find out that you each want very different things in life.

You now hold the other team's playbook and can see what makes men do what they do and not do what they don't do. This is crucial information because you have to understand that which you are pursuing or that which you are interacting with. Men will not approach situations the way you do, but understanding how they approach the situations that are relevant to your relationship will be priceless to you.

Knowing how to interact is a huge part of your strategy. Once that's done, you have to practice those skills so that you can apply them and generate the results you want. With the right communication know-how, you can learn how to physically, mentally and emotionally engage a man in an authentic and genuine way. **You are going to be a knockout.** Each and every one of you has a unique challenge and a unique set of skills. From the get-go, I cautioned you not to lose sight of the fact that you do not have to have a man to be happy in your life. But if having a man is nonetheless what you want, then I've given you the tools to achieve that.

I believe we create what we want in this world. We create the script of our lives. Are you sick of my saying that? Good. I hope that means you've got it down and are ready to write the outcome you want. My goal was to teach you to master the game called love. I know that you can change your mind-set to that of a winner, because you are a winner. You're at the end of the book, but hopefully just getting started on a more fulfilling life. Throughout, I've had you roll up your sleeves and do some work. Maybe you didn't always like taking such an honest, even brutal, look at yourself. Maybe the candid revelations I asked you to make about yourself were tough to swallow. But I bet they opened your eyes. You've heard me say lots of times that the difference between winners and losers is that winners do things that losers do not want to do. If you've followed this book, then you've done a lot of those things. You've taken a good hard look at yourself, asked yourself some tough questions and drilled deep to answer them. You were honest with yourself about your strengths and weaknesses, and you gave serious thought to what you want, what you don't want and what you absolutely will not tolerate. You've created a vision for your life. I'd put money on it that you know yourself better right now than you did when you were standing in line at the bookstore.

After you do all this, your relationships change—not just your relationships with men, but your relationship with yourself.

You discover the parts of yourself that any man would want. You see that you have value. You're worthy. You won't settle for less than you deserve, and you won't settle for less just because you want somebody—anybody—to want you.

By now, you know that Jerry Maguire's mumbo jumbo about "you complete me" is bogus. Nobody completes anybody. We complete ourselves. You don't have to have somebody else to be whole. When you discover all that, boyfriend or no boyfriend, you have changed and your life has changed.

Get ready! People will respond to you differently and you will attract what you want in your life. I'm confident that you will find the guy who has the Character of Him to go with the Character of You and that you will gravitate toward a man who matches your sense of personal worthiness. As I said from the start, my goal is to help you stop kissing frogs and wasting valuable time. And you obviously had it with those frogs yourself, because you picked up this book. Maybe by the time you're reading this, you've found your prince or someone who's got potential to wear that crown. He's your Mr. 80 Percent. Well then, good for you. I'm happy for you and I'll see you at the wedding. But if you haven't, then you've got the plan and strategy to find him. I also thought it was crucial to talk to you about the tools you need to keep that relationship as strong as possible and how to move things along if it gets stalled. The dating world hasn't gotten any easier. It hasn't changed since you started reading this book, but your knowledge about it has. You know how to go for what you want. You've got the training, the insight and the plan to find him, bag him and take him home.

I stand by what I said in some of the first pages of this book: I believe with great certainty that the special someone who can light you up from the inside out exists. People say, "Relationships are made in heaven." That may be true on some level, but relationships are managed on earth. And you live on earth. Just as we create the scripts of our lives, we create our relationships.

The bottom line is that loving smart means believing in yourself, your worth and your value. I don't want you to settle for cloud eight when you can be on cloud nine. Remember, if you think you are a prize egg, you are going to hold out for someone who is a prize egg and can appreciate another prize egg. That's the way to raise your game and play it right. You pulled over, put yourself in the "relationship shop" and made the repairs needed to create a smooth and rewarding ride through the rest of your life. YOU are the driver and no longer the passenger waiting to see where the road takes you. Enjoy, and God bless.

And on a cold winter's night a lonely dog howled at a distant moon.

About the Author

PHILLIP C. McGRAW, PH.D., is the #1 *New York Times* bestselling author of *Family First: Your Step-by-Step Plan for Creating a Phenomenal Family, The Ultimate Weight Solution, Self Matters, Relationship Rescue* and *Life Strategies*. The host of the nationally syndicated daily one-hour series *Dr. Phil*, Dr. McGraw is one of the world's foremost experts in the field of human functioning. He and his wife have been loving smart for thirty years and have two grown sons who reflect it.